"Frank Turner is a gift to the Kingdom of God. This book is perhaps his greatest work. It is a transparent look into his struggle and a powerful witness of his triumphant deliverance. After reading this book, you will be convinced of the power of a singular testimony. This is a must-read, and I pray it blesses you as it has blessed me."

Bishop Joseph W. Walker III
Senior Pastor
Mount Zion Baptist Church
Nashville, Tennessee

"In his first book, *Rapture Your Destiny*, Frank Turner Jr. asked the question: what is your purpose in life? He then answered that question with a carefully thought out meditation from the Word of God. In this second book, *Breaking the Curse*, he takes it a step further. He is asking what obstacles in a person's life would keep him or her from progressing toward that God-given destiny.

"Frank is a student of the Scriptures. May this new book speak to your heart … just as God has spoken to his."

Richard B. Anderson,
Headmaster
Christ Presbyterian Academy
Nashville, Tennessee
SOLI DEO GLORIA
To God Alone Be the Glory

"Frank Turner's story is powerful. He has traveled through the fire and into God's light. We need to listen to him. *Breaking the Curse* is a book everyone should read. It is packed with startling facts, filled with inspiration, and infused with God's love."

Rev. Erie Chapman,
MTS, JD,
Former federal prosecutor and past
president and CEO, Baptist Hospital
Nashville, Tennessee

"I want to personally write and recommend Frank Turner Jr.'s book *Breaking the Curse from a Twisted Life.* There is no better way to learn how to overcome addiction except from an addict. This is a personal testimony as well as a practical guide for those who find themselves enslaved due to the past decisions of their life. It is written simply and to the point. Everything I read in the book is in harmony with the traditions and experiences of those who are professionals in this area. As a pastor, I fully recommend Mr. Turner's book to those in need."

Pastor Gary Allen Henecke
Nashville First Church
of the Nazarene
Nashville, Tennessee

Breaking the Curse From a Twisted Life

Bad Habits, Addictions, and the Generational Curse

Frank Turner Jr.

WestBow
PRESS
A DIVISION OF THOMAS NELSON

WestBow Press books may be ordered through booksellers or by contacting:

WestBow Press
A Division of Thomas Nelson
1663 Liberty Drive
Bloomington, IN 47403
www.westbowpress.com
1-(866) 928-1240

ISBN: 978-1-4497-1638-7 (sc)
ISBN: 978-1-4497-1639-4 (hc)
ISBN: 978-1-4497-1637-0 (e)

Library of Congress Control Number: 2011927539

Printed in the United States of America

WestBow Press rev. date: 02/27/2012

Lord, keep me from the path of the destroyer,
and bless me to recognize the dream-killers ... Amen!

CONTENTS

A TWISTED LIFE

While growing up as a child, I would notice at times certain people doing immoral things. At the time, I was actually too young to know that some things were immoral, but one way or another I knew they were awkward and stood out for some reason.

I would then say to myself, "I'm never going to be like that when I grow up." Yet, I've found myself in certain vices that seemed to have crept up on me out of nowhere in my life's journey. I can remember seeing people staggering drunk and saying, "Why don't they just stop drinking?" as though to stop was easy as flicking a light switch off and it would be over.

All I did know when I was young was that life seemed like it was fun, peaceful, and adventurous, but somewhere along the way, it became twisted—out of control!

What child, when asked what he or she would like to be when he or she grows up, would raise his or her hand and say, "I would like to be a corrupt business person, dishonest politician, drug addict, prostitute, or lifelong criminal in prison"?

Yet in all reality, we are born into a world that has an extremely hostile environment, and this environment is visual and destructive. It is visual to the extent that most of its observers become a product of their atmosphere.

We not only see the destructiveness of an assortment of dishonesty, corruption, and immorality, but many are the victims of this twisted life. There are victims on both ends of the continuum. On one end, there is a way of life that suggest to get by the best way you can, fair is when the results benefit you by any means possible and at whatever cost. The other end is the person who has reaped the undeserved consequences of the abuse of the person who is twisted.

With all of this being said, one has to contemplate what has gone wrong. Whether it's your community, neighborhood, friend, or family, what is the source of such confusion, and is there a solid remedy if one is ready to change one's life for the better?

There will be some people who will oppose the contents of this book because of unbelief in spiritual reality. But for others, this will be an educational experience packed with the power to change a twisted life to a straight, productive path of meaning, purpose, and love.

The true essence of life is spiritual reality, spiritual meaning that there are invisible phenomena that exist and reality meaning that they are real. For an example, our thoughts are invisible—we can't taste, touch, or smell them—but we know they exist because of the volatile movement that's in our mind when we are thinking. Our emotions are felt, but you can't physically touch them because they are invisible. We also can see the leaves shaking on a tree when the wind is blowing, which is the effect of the wind, but no one has actually seen the wind. These are only a few tangible examples of the invisible authenticity of spiritual reality. Whether you choose to believe it or not, these intrinsic values in every human were designed and created by God, and they can interact with other celestial powers. Understanding this is where the breaking of curses, the change of bad habits, and the healing of addiction begin.

Every human being comes into this world a spiritual being with the desire to be loved and accepted. When this spiritual appetite is not allowed to be properly nurtured by God, a person will began to fill that desire with another person, place, craze, object, or action with the purpose of gratifying that contentment to be loved and accepted. The fact is that most people do this without even realizing it; as a result, bad habits develop because they will continue to repeat the action subconsciously in search for love, contentment, and the meaning of life.

Human beings are creatures of habit. Habits are going to develop anyway because that's our nature. With the understanding of this innate behavior, people should want to put forth the effort to discipline themselves into developing good habits. If not, bad habits will form. In other words, habits are going to emerge anyway, so if we develop them willingly and with focus, good ones will take place, or if we don't, bad ones will breed.

We all should know that this universe and earth are just too sophisticated to have popped out of nowhere or evolved on their own. Common sense informs us that's ridiculous. The law of physics state that for every action, there is a counter reaction—up vs. down, in vs. out, left vs. right, etc. So just the fact that we live on this earth and the way it functions is evident that the action to the counter reaction of life on earth had to be well thought out, planned, and created by an entity more incredible and greater than the human imagination.

Not only is that true, but there is also an opposing force to God and His human race, which is the source of the counter reaction of bad habits. Most bad habits culminate into an addiction, which in turn can cause a person to be bound in a spiritual curse.

Some bad habits are inherited from our family tree, while others are developed through undisciplined behavior or a person's environmental culture. When these negative virtues are not harnessed, they can lead to bad health, mental illness, prison, premature death, broken relationships, assault, and various other violent crimes, even suicide and murder.

The purpose of this book is to help a person get right down to the root cause of a personal issue that seems to keep him or her snagged or stuck in life. It is to assist him or her into moving to the next level of purpose, peace, and well being while equipping him or her with the tools to be a light so others whose life may seem trapped can see the way out.

The material that is covered in this book is also vital for the continual overcoming victory of addictions. *Webster's Dictionary*[1] defines addiction as, "To [surrender] one's self habitually or compulsively." This includes anything from substance abuse, and as I've already clarified, uncontrollable conduct (bad habits). One of the most amazing things to know and that is important for your individual personal management is that the foundation of an addict is in every human being. If you are alive and breathing, the foundation of addiction is in you. Of course, this certainly does not mean that every human being is an addict—because they're not. The foundation of being or becoming an addict is a *heart* issue. The spiritual heart is what defines every person's passions, and every person has a spiritual heart. Without knowing your authentic identity and the spiritual assets available to you, it's extremely difficult to release your passions effectively for the good of yourself and others. Without knowing your authenticity, it's most likely that your heart could be full of the wrong passions to pursue your (*right*) purpose in life, right purpose meaning your date with destiny, because your birth was not an accident. Everything God created has a specific purpose. Your life is not just for you to take up space on earth for no reason other than to live. As a result, different addictions can unfold because you're not in your meaningful purpose, and this is a tactic of God's enemy to keep you confused, distracted, and bound by a curse. *There is a God-given purpose for your life!*

---

1   Merriam Webster's Dictionary & Thesaurus (addiction).

The thief cometh not, but for to steal, and to kill, and to destroy: I am come that they might have life, and that they might have *it* more abundantly (John 10:10 KJV).

CHAPTER ONE

WHAT IS A CURSE?

Dictionary.com an online dictionary define the word curse as follows:

a) The expression of a wish that misfortune, evil, doom, etc., befall someone.

b) A formula or charm intended to cause such misfortune to another.

c) The act of reciting such formula.

d) A profane or obscene word, esp. as used in anger or for emphasis; swearword.

The Bible is a book that has stood the test of time from generation to generation. It is historically proven that people have lived by it and nations have self-destructed because of its neglect. The wisdom of the Bible is notoriously mesmerizing, for in it resides the questions and answers of life.

The original languages in the Bible for the Old Testament are Hebrew and Aramaic, while the unique communication for the New Testament is Greek; these languages or more definitive than the English language, definitive meaning that they give more detail.

In Hebrew, the word אָרַר, pronounced *'ārar*, means to curse. This root is found in South Arabic, Ethiopic, and Akkadian.[1] The verb occurs sixty times in the Old Testament, and its English equivalent is to execrate. Execrate means to declare to be evil or detestable and corresponds to the letter a in the above definition. This kind of curse also can be directed at a

---

1   All three definitions of the word (curse) are from the Vine's Expository Dictionary of Old and New Testament Words. Word Search 7 Multi-Media Bible Software

person when someone literally talks down and says bad, destructive things about somebody, either audibly or in the quietness of their thoughts.

קָלַל *qālal,* means to be trifling, light, and swift; to curse. It frequently includes the idea of "cursing" or scorning or mocking; to bring into contempt; afflict as in the letter d in the above definition. It's when verbal profanity is spoken toward someone. Stated in inner-city syntax, it's when you get cussed out! The word occurs about eighty-two times in the Hebrew Old Testament.

The word, אָלָה *'ālâ,* is another Hebrew word for curse and is used as a noun. In distinction from *'ārar* ("to proclaim evil") and *qālal* ("to curse by abusing or by belittling"), *'ālâ* basically refers to "the execution of a proper oath to legalize a covenant or agreement." In essence, the noun *ālâ* in ancient biblical times meant that evil would come upon a person if he or she made a promise or entered a covenant with someone and didn't keep it. It also consists of proclaiming an oath against someone as in the letters b and c in the above definition, which is knowingly instituting evil misfortune and destruction on someone.

So the word curse as noun and verb renders different Hebrew words, some of them being more or less synonymous, differing only in degree of strength. It is often used in contrast with "bless" or "blessing" (see Deut. 11:29). When a curse is pronounced against any person, we are not to understand this as a mere wish, however violent, that disaster should overtake the person in question, any more than we are to understand that a corresponding "blessing" conveys simply a wish that prosperity should be the lot of the person on whom the blessing is invoked. A curse was considered to possess an inherent power of carrying itself into effect.

Prayer has been defined as a wish referred to God. Curses (or blessings) were imprecations referred to supernatural beings in whose existence and power to do well or inflict harm primitive man believed. The use of magic and spells of all kinds is based on the belief that it is possible to enlist the support of supernatural beings with whom the universe abounds, and to persuade them to carry out the suppliant's wishes. It has been suggested that spells were written on pieces of parchment (paper made of sheep skin) and cast to the winds in the belief that they would find their way to their proper destination—that some demonic being would act as postman and deliver them at the proper address.[2]

---

2   *International Standard Bible Encyclopedia* [curse] (Word Search 7 Multi-Media Bible Software).

So basically a curse is when someone expresses or evokes evil on someone. It can come in a variety of ways. Some people may choose to think that this is very silly and only a myth. But in reality, if you just look at the world news, it's easy to see that something a little more destructive than bad luck is happening. Of course, I personally choose not to believe in luck. However, there are good times and bad times. There is also evidence of an invisible pressure that seems to be thwarting some people's lives.

This ill fortune has had a traumatic affect on society for centuries —ever since the beginning of the world, as a matter of fact. First of all, we have to come to the realization that Almighty God is a true, real, living reality. Once we come to grips with this absolute truth, then it's not hard to understand that God also has an enemy. The Creator of the universe has established spiritual laws that govern this earth. If they are violated by any person, it opens the door to be vulnerable to the Creator's enemy. Therefore, one of the many ways a person can become a victim of circumstance is by violating God's laws. This is not to say that every act or move a person makes will result in experiencing a curse, but we do need to pay close attention to a continual negative pattern or lifestyle.

We must also consider that accidents do happen, so a sudden misfortune may or may not be the consequences of a curse. However, the result of a continual lifestyle that ignores God causes a person to experience various curses. These curses have a domino effect and can pass over into a family and flow through it from generation to generation until the family dynasty is destroyed or the curse is broken. And if it does escape a person's family, it still can affect society, including a person's career, because of someone else's neglect. The domino effect of cursed humanity can even affect the forces of nature, causing cataclysmic disaster.

> The earth also was corrupt before God, and the earth was filled with violence. And God looked upon the earth, and, behold, it was corrupt; for all flesh had corrupted his way upon the earth.
>
> And, behold, I, even I, do bring a flood of waters upon the earth, to destroy all flesh, wherein *is* the breath of life, from under heaven; *and* everything that *is* in the earth shall die (Gen 6:11–12, 17 KJV).

When a person is not exposed to and in relationship with Almighty God, he or she does not have access to the resources to rule over the curse.

3

If you choose to believe that this is not true, then you are making yourself vulnerable to be the victim of a curse out of ignorance. And the most dangerous thing in the world is to be ignorant of your ignorance. I'm sure you have a friend or loved one who may be having habitual problems in life. Stay with this book if you want help.

Not being in Christ will open the door for people to be manipulated by evil forces. Any person in this position does not have the weapons that are designed by God and needed to be affective in overcoming and/or resisting this moral evil. It's like getting caught inside of a whirlwind or a tornado that will cause you to land in several rough places throughout life, maybe even a premature death. The Bible says:

> The fear of the Lord is the beginning of [wisdom]; and the knowledge of the holy is understanding. For by me thy days shall be *multiplied*, and the *years* of the *life* shall be increased (Prov. 9:10–11 KJV emphasis mine).

Christ came into this world to give us life, but the main motive of God's enemy is to steal, kill, and destroy us (see John 10:10). The danger is that most people who are the victim of a curse don't realize it while the curse is happening. All they know is that it seems like nothing they set out to accomplish comes to fruition unless it is something selfish and self-gratifying. The end result of the selfish self-gratification is a deceptive, coercive tactic of the enemy. Temptations originate from our own ungodly inner desires but are created by God's enemy.

> Let no man say when he is tempted, I am tempted of God: for God cannot be tempted with evil, neither tempteth he any man: But every man is tempted when he is drawn away of his own lust, and enticed. Then when lust is conceived, it bringeth forth sin: and sin, when it is finished, bringeth forth death. (James 1:13-15 KJV)

You should already know that if God's enemy tried to entice Jesus, he will also entice you (see Matt. 4:1–11). This foe uses these enticements and temptations as bait to lure us into various curses. And in the long run, this selfish fruit leads to destruction. It may seem that you are never able to grasp and hold on to the good things in life. The most powerful good thing in life is to have the peace of God in your heart, to love, to be loved, and to know that you can make a difference in the world and someone else's life.

Money can't buy these things. Only God can give them. It doesn't matter who you are, what type of education you posses, or how much money and clout you may have—at some point, you just realize that something in your life is missing. Without Jesus, the true meaning, contentment, and purpose of existing are not present in your heart.

Living in the curse makes a person have a wrong perception about life. It is false evidence appearing real. It appears real because of the illusion that's played out in the mind's eye. When a person believes a lie, it appears real because it has become part of his or her belief system. Thoughts become words, words become action, and action becomes character, and the fruit of your character leads you to your destiny, *for better or worse.* The wrong ideas planted into your belief system will lead you to destruction. Because of the physical movement to and from, day in and day out, it seems like you may be accomplishing something in life, only to find out months and in some cases years later that the only thing that has changed is your age. You may then come to realize that the meaning and purpose of your life has been stagnant. Some people are lonely and have no friends. They may even die old and all alone because of the lie of life that's in their mind's eye if they live through life long enough looking for a place called there that doesn't even exist.

A lot of young people find themselves involved in gangs, murder, drugs, and incarceration as a result of living in the curse. They are full of bitterness and anger. Some are totally mad at the world. Many do not even love themselves. Part of the effect of certain curses is that people don't even realize that they don't love themselves. They may think they do, but their lifestyle shows they don't. If you don't love yourself, it is totally impossible to love someone else. And when they do love, their hatred is stronger than their love because their emotions are out of balance.

When people are spiritually out of balance, they can easily confuse infatuation with the opposite sex (and some people the same sex) for love. It is also easy to replace the emotional pain of rejection with an arrogant, prideful attitude of violence in order to be accepted by others. This is part of the delusional lie that's subtly accepted into a person's belief system as a result of a curse.

I know that these may seem like some hard statements. But we have to come to grips with the absolute truth of the Bible if we are going to experience deliverance and divine healing.

> You must understand this: In the last days there will be violent periods of time. People will be selfish and love money. They will brag, be arrogant, and use abusive language. They will [curse] their parents, show no gratitude, have no respect for what is holy, and lack normal affection for their families. They will refuse to make peace with anyone. They will be slanderous, lack self-control, be brutal, and have no love for what is good. They will be traitors. They will be reckless and conceited. *They will love pleasure rather than God.* They will appear to have a godly life, **but they will not let its power change them.** Stay away from such people. Some of these men go into homes and mislead weak-minded women who are burdened with sins and led by all kinds of desires. These women are always studying but are never able to recognize the truth ... Having eyes full of adultery, and that cannot cease from sin; beguiling unstable souls: an heart they have exercised with covetous practices; [cursed] children (2 Tim. 3:1–7, God's Word; 2 Peter 2:14 KJV, emphasis mine).

These Scriptures give a word picture of how some people's lives look while living in or experiencing the curse. And we do see this type of character and activity all around us in our society today. Another type or form of a curse is in the atmosphere. As I said earlier, there are spiritual laws that God has established that play its part in governing the earth. It is possible that the consequences of this type of curse can rest in the wood, stone, and concrete of your house when you become the victim of it.

> I looked up again and saw a flying scroll. The angel asked me, "What do you see?" "I see a flying scroll," I answered. "It's 30 feet long and 15 feet wide." Then he said to me, "This is a [curse] that will go out all *over the earth.* The one side of the scroll says that every [thief] will be forced away. The other side of the scroll says that everyone who takes an oath will be forced away. I will send out a [curse], declares the Lord of Armies, and it will enter the [houses] of [thieves] and the [houses] of those who take oaths in my name. *It will stay in their houses and destroy the timber and stone.*" I will bring it forth, saith the LORD of hosts, and it shall enter into the house of the thief, and into the

house of him that sweareth falsely by my name: and it shall remain in the midst of his house, and shall consume it with the timber thereof and the stones thereof (Zech. 5:1–4 God's Word, emphasis mine).

Remember that earlier we talked about how in ancient times, curses were written on parchment and cast into the air. In this passage of Scripture, the Bible talks about an angel speaking with Zechariah the prophet. He was describing a curse as a result of lying (swearing falsely) as well as stealing that was written in a scroll. A scroll is a roll of parchment that was usually used for a book. But this one was extremely large, thirty feet long and fifteen feet wide. On one side of the scroll was written the sanction for violating the third of the Ten Commandments, which was taking God's name in vain (swearing falsely, see Exod. 20:7). On the other side was written the violation of the eighth commandment, which was, "Thou shalt not steal" (Exod. 20:15). This curse would rest in a person's house, affecting his or her family and in some cases possibly the friends who visit him or her.

Just think about how many people use the phrase, "I swear to God" or as the younger generation says, "I put that on everything I love," not realizing the burden that they are bringing on themselves.

But I say unto you, Swear not at all; neither by heaven; for it is God's throne: Nor by the earth; for it is his footstool: neither by Jerusalem; for it is the city of the great King. Neither shalt thou swear by thy head, because thou canst not make one hair white or black. But let your communication be, Yea, yea; Nay, nay: for whatsoever is more than these cometh of evil (Matt. 5:34–37 KJV).

There is a saying, "Ignorance of the law is no excuse." That should especially go toward God's law, which is the mother of all laws. Of course, you should already know that thieves are people who just flat out steal. But also look at the consequences they bring on themselves. Wherever they eat, sleep, and rest, their head is doomed because they do not know of the curse. Another food for thought is the people in the business world who are dishonest in their dealings. Any type of negotiation that's dishonest is stealing. It doesn't matter who you are or how slick you may think you can get—God knows your thoughts and motives.

O Lord, you have examined me, and you know me. You alone know when I sit down and when I get up. You read my thoughts from far away. You watch me when I travel and when I rest. You are familiar with all my ways. Even before there is a [single] word on my tongue, you know all about it, Lord. You are all around me—in front of me and in back of me. You lay your hand on me. Such knowledge is beyond my grasp. It is so high I cannot reach it (Ps. 139:1–6 God's Word).

Something else that's in the atmosphere that we must consider is the curse from wickedness. Listen to what else the angel explained to the prophet Zechariah.

Then the angel that talked with me went forth, and said unto me, Lift up now thine eyes, and see what is this that goeth forth. And I said, What is it? And he said, This is an ephah (*a basket*) that goeth forth. He said moreover, This is their resemblance through all the earth. And, behold, there was lifted up a talent of lead: and this is a woman that sitteth in the midst of the ephah. And he said, This is [*wickedness*]. And he cast it into the midst of the ephah; and he cast the weight of lead upon the mouth thereof. Then lifted I up mine eyes, and looked, and, behold, there came out two women, and the wind was in their wings; for they had wings like the wings of a stork: and they lifted up the ephah between the earth and the heaven (*in the air*). Then said I to the angel that talked with me, Whither do these bear the ephah? And he said unto me, To build it an house in the land of Shinar and it shall be established, and set there upon her own base (Zech. 5:5–11 KJV emphasis mine)

Shinar is a word for Babylon that means confusion. The nation of Babylon was a physical ancient world empire whose character became a metaphor for the habitation of evil. This city is spoken about in the book of Revelation. It is a spiritual city of ungodliness.

Babylon the Great ... She has become a home for demons. She is a [prison] for every evil spirit, every unclean bird, and every unclean and hated beast. (Revelation 18:2 God's Word)

WHAT IS A CURSE?

The unclean bird is a metaphor for demons. Also, the mythical animal (beast) symbolizes an evil spirit.[3] This basket that's spoken about in the above passages has its foundation in the spiritual city Babylon (confusion), confusion being when a person is spiritually out of balance, as we talked about earlier. The basket symbolizes that the boundaries of the curse from wickedness cannot be loosed unless the legal spiritual laws of God are broken by a disobedient lifestyle. The curse of wickedness does influence the whole world because it lives in the atmosphere and coerces wickedness throughout the world but cannot be effective unless obeyed. When a person willfully disobeys God's standard of life, he or she can ignorantly be manipulated by wickedness and experience the curse. This is how the curse is obeyed. The spiritual city (Babylon) also has a prince who has power in the air.

> Wherein in time past ye walked according to the course of
> this world, according to the *prince of the power of the air*, the
> spirit that now worketh in the children of disobedience …
> (Eph. 2:2 KJV emphasis mine).

The prince of the power of the air is none other than the devil himself. In other words, society that ignores Almighty God is where the devil's throne is, and a throne is a place of rulership. This position is where the spiritual city Babylon (confusion) exists. There are countless people who are dominated by these various curses and don't even realize it— from individuals to families to businesses to politicians, which results in corrupt politics. Even in certain countries of the world the whole nation is subjugated to satanic oppression.

As I said earlier, just because a person does something wrong or ungodly doesn't mean that he or she is going to be taken out by a curse. God is not some tyrant on a throne with a spiritual baseball bat waiting on you to make a mistake. The devil may be (John 10:10a), but God isn't. Just please do consider if there is something in your life that's morally wrong and has a habitual grip on you, then you may need some godly spiritual counseling.

People who are living outside of the boundaries God has established to govern the human race are living in disobedience. The disobedience that is spoken about in Ephesians 2:2 is referring to those who are not saved by the blood of Jesus Christ. The mother sin of all sins is refusing Jesus

---

3   *Dictionary of Biblical Imagery* (mythical animals pg. 578)

as Lord and Master of your life. The fullness of God's Commandment to the world says:

> And this is His commandment: that we should believe on the name of His Son Jesus Christ and love one another, as He gave us commandment (1 John 3:23 KJV).

To ignore this commandment is flat-out disobedience, and it leaves a person without the blessing and weapons to overcome the curse. God loves the human race so much that He gave us a mind to think for ourselves when He created us. This love for us is so deep that He created the whole universe to support our physical existence. You should read my book entitled *Rapture Your Destiny* for an in-depth revelation on how the universe functions in harmony with the human race. Everything in the universe works in harmony and synchronization except for a large portion of the human race, and that's because God gave us the right to freedom of choice. If you force someone to love you, you won't be able to tell if his or her freedom of choice is to really love you or not. So God, who is love, gave us this option to see who would really choose to love Him. Even though God knows everything, there are people who will choose not to obey His command or love Him, as in the case of Cain.

> And the Lord said unto Cain, Why are you angry? and why is your face sad? If you do well will you not have honor? And if you do wrong sin (*the curse*) is waiting at the door, desiring to have you, *but don't let it be your master* (Gen. 4:6, 7 Bible in Basic English, emphasis mine).

Cain, who had the freedom of choice just as we do, chose to have a cold attitude toward God and continued a lifestyle of disobedience. This was because his younger brother was experiencing the blessings of God as a result of faith and obedience, which made Cain jealous. This willful act of arrogance opened the door for him to be influenced by the enemy, who used the tool of wickedness to drive him. As a result, he murdered his brother Abel (see Gen. 4:8).

God admired Abel because he believed and possibly understood the promise of God, which was the prophecy of the coming of Jesus Christ, the promised seed (see Gen. 3:15). His faith proved this when he offered up a sacrifice that was symbolic of the sacrifice of Jesus the Messiah:

> And Abel, he also brought of the firstlings of his flock and
> of the fat thereof. And the Lord had respect unto Abel and
> to his offering (Gen. 4:4 KJV).

So, just like Cain, who put himself in the curse because of his arrogance (see Gen. 4:9–11), people today will chose to disobey God's command. The command is to believe in the good news of the promised seed, and some will even get a violent attitude about it. The Bible is very clear that the mother of all sins is unbelief in Jesus Christ. Unbelief makes a person a victim of the curse and a citizen of the demonic spiritual city Babylon.

I will be discussing a little more about the spiritual city of Babylon later in the book. However absurd this may sound, today's society cannot and must not rule out the fact that this morally evil, spiritual city is real.

Again I want to say that the Bible is very clear that the mother of all sins is unbelief in Jesus Christ.

> Neither is there salvation in any other: for there is none
> other name under heaven given among men, whereby we
> must be saved...

Neither repented (changed their mind) they of their murders, nor of their sorceries (drug use), nor of their fornication (public sex and its abuse), nor of their thefts (Acts 4:12; Rev. 9:21 KJV emphasis mine).

CHAPTER TWO

THE HISTORY OF CURSES

Words are a medium by which thoughts are expressed; as Pastor Michael L. Sweat says, "Everything begins with a thought."[1]

The utterance that is spoken by every human being originates in the heart and is rationalized through the mind before it comes out of the mouth. And then there are other instances when the mind influences the heart and a person will speak it out. Actually, this phenomenon is quite simple to understand because we all do it. Everyone has become accustomed to it because it is a process of human function. We do it without even realizing it; as a matter of fact, it shouldn't be hard to grasp that concept. It's just plain ole common sense.

But the amazing thing is to understand that every human being was created in the image of God. The Bible declares that everything in existence came from the spoken word or better yet, the voice of God. In basic terminology, the physical things in the world that we see with our natural eyes had to be in the heart of God and thought out in His mind before He spoke it. Then when He spoke it—it came into reality.

The person who chooses not to believe this is indirectly calling God a liar. We know that God spoke the world into existence because He told us He did. The Bible is the written Word of God's spoken Word. Those who are born-again believers know that the written Word of God says that He verbally spoke the universe into existence. The Bible says:

> Through faith we understand that the worlds were framed by the [word] of God, so that things which are [seen] were not

---

1   Michael L Sweat Pastor of Praise God Ministries Nashville, Tennessee.

made of things which do [appear] (Heb. 11:3 KJV emphasis mine).

And God [said], "Let there be light …" (Gen. 1:3).

And God [said], "Let there be a firmament" (Gen. 1:6).

And God [said], "Let the waters under heaven be gathered to one place …" (Gen. 1:9).

And God [said], "Let the earth bring forth grass …" (Gen. 1:11).

And God [said], "Let there be lights in the firmament …" (Gen. 1:14).

And God [said], "Let the waters bring forth abundantly …" (Gen. 1:20).

And God [said], "Let us make man in our image …" (Gen. 1:26).

Everything came into being at the command of God. When God commanded creation to come forth, He included the spiritual laws that govern the universe. Violation of these spiritual laws has ramifications that lead to certain consequences. Of course, we all know that included in the universe is this planet called Earth.

God, who is the creator of all things, is the first to proclaim curses. After God created the first man, He commanded him not to eat from the tree of the knowledge of good and evil. He warned the man of the consequences of eating from the tree. "In the day that you eat of it you shall surely die," He said (Genesis 2:16–17). The biblical definition of death does not mean the end of the sensation of life. We're created in God's image, and our true essences are soul and spirit. Just as God, who is Spirit (John 4:24), lives forever, our spirit and soul will also live forever. What a person does with Jesus on this side of death determines where his or her spirit and soul will spend eternity.[2] The biblical definition of death means separation. That's why when you go to a funeral or see a dead person his or her body looks like it does, because the actual person is not inside of it anymore (2 Cor. 5:8). The person (his or her soul and spirit) has been separated from the body that housed him or her.

The main point is that what God commanded, He spoke, and it happened and is still happening today. People are dying every day as a

---

2   Matthew 7:21–23 (KJV).

result of Adam and Eve's disobedience. When God confronted them concerning their disobedience Adam pointed to Eve, and Eve blamed the serpent, which was the body the devil (an evil spirit) was inside of.[3] It was in judgment against the devil that God Himself announced the first curse in history.

> And the Lord God said unto the serpent, Because thou has done this, thou are [cursed] above all cattle, and every beast of the field; upon thy belly shalt thou go, and dust shalt thou eat all the days of thy life: And I will put enmity between thee and the woman, and between thy seed and her seed; it shall bruise thy head, and thou shalt bruise his heel (Gen. 3:14–15 KJV).

The next curse was decreed against the man, the woman, and the ground that God had created.

> Unto the woman he said, I will greatly multiply thy sorrow and thy conception; in sorrow thou shalt bring forth children; and thy desire shall be to thy husband, and he shall rule over thee.
>
> And unto Adam he said, Because thou hast hearkened unto the voice of thy wife, and hast eaten of the tree, of which I commanded thee, saying, Thou shalt not eat of it: [cursed] is the ground for thy sake; in sorrow shalt thou eat of it all the days of thy life;
>
> Thorns also and thistles shall it bring forth to thee; and thou shalt eat the herb of the field;
>
> In the sweat of thy face shalt thou eat bread, till thou return unto the ground; for out of it wast thou taken: for dust thou art, and unto dust shalt thou return (Gen. 3:16–19 KJV).

God proclaimed these curses as judgment because of disobedience, judgment meaning that justice is done as a sanction to a moral situation. The judgment of God or the activity in response to His spiritual laws of a moral decision can be favorable or non-favorable. In this case, it was non-favorable. The word moral means right or wrong behavior sanctioned by

---

3   Genesis 3:9–13 (KJV).

the voice of your conscience or ethical decision. Our conscience is the voice of our human spirit and works in synchronization with the mind that is the master control center for the spirit, soul, and body. And one of the most awesome things to realize is that the law of God is written in every human being's heart.[4] We all know right from wrong, but we all don't choose to do what is right all of the time.

Also, we all know that God Himself is a holy God; the word holy means free from moral evil. In other words, God does not do any evil whatsoever, because He is holy. *So the curses were proclaimed to warn of the danger of violating God's spiritual laws and the consequences of living a life outside of an intimate relationship with God—our Creator.*

Because of the disobedience of eating from the tree of the knowledge of good and evil, the first humans were separated from the presence of God, which is what spiritual death is. This defiance made them the enemy of God because it included their innate possession of the knowledge of evil, which began to live in their hearts. The dwelling of evil in the heart put them at enmity with God. This malady of spiritual genetics was passed on to every human who has been born into this world, because we're all descendants of the first Man and Woman. *Therefore, we come into this world separated from God and with the effect of the curse on us and all around us.*

There are three elements of the curse in Scripture:

(a) Against the created order,
(b) In interpersonal relationships,
(c) And the consequences of neglecting and/or ignoring God's covenant.

(a) Against the created order: the human race is the highest order of species God created. We're even created in His image. Within the depth of His love, we, having been created in His image, were granted dominion over the earth.[5] As a result, the human lifestyle has a tremendous impact on the elements of the earth and all of creation. In other words, how we act has a domino effect on creation, clean down to the forces of nature.

> And God saw that the wickedness of man was great in the earth, and that every [imagination] of the [thoughts] of his heart was only evil continually. And it repented the LORD that he had made man on the earth, and it grieved him at his heart.

4   Romans 2:14–15 (KJV).
5   Genesis 1:28 (KJV).

> And the LORD said, I will destroy man whom I have created from the face of the earth; both man, and beast, and the creeping thing, and the fowls of the air; for it repenteth me that I have made them…
>
> The earth also was corrupt before God, and the earth was filled with violence.
>
> And God looked upon the earth, and, behold, it was corrupt; for all flesh had corrupted his way upon the earth.
>
> And God said unto Noah, The end of all flesh is come before me; for the earth is filled with violence through them; and, behold, *I will destroy them with the earth* (Gen, 6:5–7, 11–13 KJV emphasis mine).

In this real-life historical event, God allowed the elements of nature to act against the human race because of their persistent wickedness of the heart.

Even though God promised to never destroy the whole world again all at the same time (see Gen. 9:15), judgment does still come by the forces of nature upon an individual, a family, a community, or a nation for the continual wickedness that they may live out every day. The curse against the created order has affected nature and man's dominion over the earth since the act of disobedience in the Garden of Eden, which caused thorns, thistles, and weeds to grow out of a perfectly tropical setting.

Even in today's reality, the inhabitants of the world encounter earthquakes, tornados, mudslides, electric thunderstorms, and a slew of other disasters. It is terribly ironic that most people overlook the fact that it's all a possible result of the continual evil and wickedness of groups of people in an area.

(b) The second element of the curse is in the area of interpersonal relationships. First it has affected human intimacy with God. As stated earlier, the whole human race is born into this world with an exceptional indifference toward God. Touching bases again in the case of Cain (murderer of his very own blood brother), because of the evil living in his heart, he still had an arrogant attitude toward God after the murder. He was extremely angry with his brother because his brother was obedient and did what was right in the sight of God.

> And in process of time it came to pass, that Cain brought of the fruit of the ground an offering unto the LORD.
>
> And Abel, he also brought of the firstlings of his flock and of the fat thereof. And the LORD had respect unto Abel and to his offering:
>
> But unto Cain and to his offering he had not respect. And Cain was very wroth (angry), and his countenance fell...
>
> And Cain talked with Abel his brother: and it came to pass, when they were in the field, that Cain rose up against Abel his brother, and slew [killed] him...
>
> And the LORD said unto Cain, Where is Abel thy brother? *And he said, I know not: Am I my brother's keeper?* (Gen. 4:3–5, 8–9 KJV emphasis mine).

Has it ever crossed your mind that when a thought comes to you to be helpful to someone, it could be God talking to you? But being ignorant or untrained to the voice of God, you answered the thought by saying, "I'm not going to help them. They need to do it themselves. After all, I got mine myself" or with some type of sarcastic answer. I'm sure there have been countless times that we all have talked crazy to God and didn't even realize it; but what about the people who do know that they are talking to God with an arrogant attitude like Cain did? This fact proves the reality of the curse affecting our intended intimacy with God.

The element of the curse that involves interpersonal relationships will not only cut people off from God but also will cut them off from other constructive people as well as cause them not to prosper from the works of their hands (see Lev. 18:29).

We have this example when God sanctioned judgment upon Cain:

> And now art thou cursed from the earth, which hath opened her mouth to receive thy brother's blood from thy hand;
>
> When thou tillest the ground, it shall not henceforth yield unto thee her strength; a fugitive and a vagabond shalt thou be in the earth (Gen. 4:11–12 KJV).

A fugitive and vagabond means that people can be a homeless wanderer in addition to other people, not wanting to be bothered with them. People just don't want to be around them and can't put their finger on why.

Another affect of cursed interpersonal relationships is the fact that some people are willfully teaming up with God's enemy, the devil! They intentionally cause problems in people's relationships and in society. They choose to do this by practicing witchcraft and black magic, as well as voodoo, etc. Not all curses are done in reference to God. These are the curses that are proclaimed by people whose wish is to do other people harm. There are some people who have made a pact with the devil in the attempt to gain power so that damage, injury, and destruction can be done to others. In the specific case of witchcraft, it is explicitly antisocial, in that it empowers and advances one individual at the expense of other individuals and the community as a whole.

The witch is only one type of practitioner of magic. Black magic is the single thread that passes through all willful demonic association. This magic is different than religion in that magic is manipulative and religion is supplicative. These, as well as several other forms of defiance of the true God, are a result of people who make a conscious appeal to Satan or his demons, which is treason— trafficking with the enemy. Rituals, mixing potions, and the act of casting spells are some of the ways these curses are implemented. Whispering or murmuring chants and sometimes speaking out loud into the air, along with the rituals and/or the mixing of potions, are how spells and collaboration with evil spirits are sanctioned. We've already learned how powerful words are. One of the most dangerous things not to know is that a curse can be pronounced against another person without even acting out rituals and mixing potions. They can, and a lot of times are, spoken out of ignorance; spoken by people who are not consciously worshiping Satan or his demons, but they are just loud-mouthed, arrogant people who spread gossip. The Bible teaches us of the power of the tongue.

> And the tongue is a fire, a world of iniquity: so is the tongue among our members, that it defileth the whole body, and setteth on [fire] the course of nature; *and it is set on fire of hell.*
>
> For every kind of beasts, and of birds, and of serpents, and of things in the sea, is tamed, and hath been tamed of mankind:

> But the tongue can no man tame; it is an unruly evil, full of deadly poison.
>
> Therewith bless we God, even the Father; and therewith [curse] we men, which are made after the similitude of God (James 3:6–9 KJV emphasis mine).

Spoken words are one of the most powerful forces in the world.

> Death and life are in the power of the tongue: and they that love it shall eat the fruit thereof (Prov. 18:21).

Another example of the power of words is when Jesus and His disciples were traveling toward Jerusalem one day, Jesus spoke to a tree, and what He said happened to the tree within twenty-four hours.

> And on the morrow, when they were come from Bethany, he was hungry:
>
> And seeing a fig tree afar off having leaves, he came, if haply he might find any thing thereon: and when he came to it, he found nothing but leaves; for the time of figs was not yet.
>
> And Jesus answered and said unto it, No man eat fruit of thee hereafter forever. And his disciples heard it...
>
> And in the morning, as they passed by, they saw the fig tree dried up from the roots.
>
> And Peter calling to remembrance saith unto him, Master, behold, the fig tree which thou [cursedst] is withered away (Mark 11:12–14; 20–21 KJV).

Please don't think that the tree withered up just because it was Jesus that was doing the speaking. This passage of Scripture teaches us that when a person believes something in his or her heart and speaks it, it will happen. This includes you, Jesus, and me.

> And Jesus answering saith unto them, Have faith in God.
>
> For verily I say unto you, That whosoever shall say unto this mountain, Be thou removed, and be thou cast into the sea; *and shall not doubt in his heart, but shall believe that those things*

which he saith shall come to pass; he shall have whatsoever he saith (Mark 11:22–23 KJV emphasis mine).

Even though Jesus is teaching His disciples as well as us to have faith in God, there is a spiritual principle that works for the better or the worse— the worse in the sense that even if a person doesn't believe in God, *it's still a spiritual law.* If people are not willfully serving God, they are insensitive to the Holy Spirit and can't control their tongue. Therefore, they speak curses into the atmosphere that affect other people. These curses are in the form of gossip, slander, and condemnation. When I look at this phenomenon, I consider how a lot of men speak negatively about women, calling them all kind of disrespectful names and obscene words. These omens that are spoken out of their mouth (because of the spiritual ignorance that's in them) causes curses to rest upon these women, making them feel emotional pain, discouragement, and low self-esteem. All of this will result in undue heaviness on their spirit and soul. Most are walking around carrying a burden on their shoulders that's as heavy as an apartment building. And when a single man meets a woman, there is a strong possibility that she could be carrying a ton of emotional baggage because his fellow man has slandered her with curses out of disrespect.

(c) The third and final element of the curse comes from the consequence of ignoring or neglecting God's covenant. A covenant is an agreement God has established for humanity to have an intimate relationship with Him. As God's appropriate response to the disobedience of His covenant, the curse threatens to deprive the violators, as well as those who ignore the reality of the existence of God, of security, freedom from bondages such as various addictions, and from inner peace, health, and blessings. But most of all, it deprives them of freedom from the dominating power of demonic manipulation and self-destruction.

Ever since ancient times, a lot of people have chosen not to pursue an intimate relationship with God. Instead, they seek to find spiritual knowledge and the meaning of life in other ways. As I've already stated, they interact with demonic spirits through false religions, witchcraft, black magic, voodoo, sorcery, divination, and other satanic worship. These forms of occultism seek to do people great harm by placing curses upon other citizens. The curses are orders given to demonic spirits by their practitioner to implement various types of destruction to their victims. Another use of satanic worship is in the attempt to manipulate natural laws to work in the person's favor who is conjuring up the evil spirits. Such beliefs and practices—principally magical or divinatory—have occurred in all human societies throughout recorded history, with considerable variations both in their nature and in the attitude of societies toward them. So basically these three categories of neglecting God carry dangerous consequences.

In the Old Testament, Israel at various times experienced curses as a chastisement for their continual idolatry (the worshiping of false gods) —a violation of the first commandment (thou shall have no other gods before me). They were constrained from enjoying certain blessings, resulting in a debasement of their God-given identity (see Exod. 20:3–6). In all actuality, experiencing the curse in ancient biblical times as well as now is a restriction of enjoying the peace, meaning, and contentment of life. It is nothing other than the reality of spiritual slavery resulting in physical stagnation, emotional frustration, incurable illnesses, and premature death. Some categories of curses are listed in the book of Deuteronomy and are still in effect today. Wherever the affected person goes, the curse follows. Here are a summary of them.

- Your food is cursed.
- The womb is barren.
- Your Garden will not grow.
- Your pets and animals will even be barren.
- You will be confused and fail in everything you do.
- Certain diseases.
- Attacks of war.
- Drought from scorching heat.
- Defeated by your enemies.
- Fear, panic, and oppression.
- Broken and adulterous engagements and marriages.
- Other people living in your house and you can't do anything about it.
- You will go mad because of the tragedy you see all around you.
- You will become a proverb and a byword among other people.

- Your children will be taken as slaves (drug use, alcohol, prostitution, human trafficking, gangs, etc.) while you watch and nothing can be done about it. You will work hard and bring in little.

- You will see others prosper as you become poorer.

The Bible says:

> All these curses shall pursue and overtake you until you are destroyed all because you refuse to listen to the Lord your God. These horrors shall befall you and your descendants as a warning:

> You will become slaves to your enemies because of your failure to praise God for all that he has given you. The Lord will send your enemies against you, and you will be hungry, thirsty, naked, and in want of everything. A yoke of iron shall be placed around your neck until you are destroyed! (Deut. 28:15–48 God's Word).

I know that this is an unpopular statement, but it's the absolute truth. The whole world is under the effect of the curse. But there is hope and victory, as we will see later on in this book.

But that's not all. We also brag when we are suffering. We know that suffering creates endurance, endurance creates character, and character creates confidence. We're not ashamed to have this confidence, because God's love has been poured into our hearts by the Holy Spirit, who has been given to us. Romans 5:3-5 (GW)

CHAPTER THREE

THE EFFECT OF CURSES

The online dictionary at www.dictionary.die.net defines the word effect as, "A phenomenon that follows and is caused by some previous phenomenon." In the book of Proverbs—which is a book of wisdom—there is a passage of Scripture that states:

> As the bird by wandering, as the swallow by flying, so the [curse] *causeless* shall not come (Prov. 26:2 KJV, emphasis mine).

So basically, the dictionary's definition of the word "effect" and the understanding of this verse out of the book of Proverbs give explanation to a spiritual principle. The principle is that for every action, there is a counteraction, such as up and down, in and out, left and right, and on and on. In other words, nothing happens unless there is something that causes it.

Have you ever stopped to think about why some of the negative things in your life are happening? This is not to say that everything that has a negative connotation is a result of a curse, but it is a good thing to do some soul-searching so you can identify the source of some of the polarizing responses that rise up against you in life. One of the steps in the twelve-step process for attaining and maintaining recovery says that a person should make a continual fearless and searching inventory of him or herself and have God remove all character defects. Please know that ignorance of a spiritual law does not show favoritism. Not doing a self-check from time to time can result in being caught up in a spiritual trap. People will always get something in response to their own actions or from the actions of another, whether good or bad. The Bible teaches that we reap what we sow.

> For he that soweth unto his own flesh shall of the flesh reap corruption; but he that soweth to the Spirit shall of the Spirit reap life everlasting (Gal. 6:8 KJV).

The biblical definition of flesh simply means when a person does things for selfish gratification and not according to the path that God has established for that physical or emotional desire to be lived out and enjoyed. The counteraction for that fleshly action—if not harnessed—would be to experience the effect of the curse. And if the trauma from that action is constantly ignored, then corruption sets in. And when corruption is full grown, it equals the death sentence.

> Let no man say when he is tempted, I am tempted of God; for God cannot be tempted with evil, and he himself tempteth no man: but each man is tempted, when he is drawn away by his own lust, and enticed. Then the lust, when it hath conceived, beareth sin: and the sin, when it is full grown, bringeth forth death (James 1:13–15 KJV).

Let's look at this phenomenon in the light of sexual promiscuity. God has created and designed sex to be enjoyed inside the institution of marriage. We all should know that. Of course, many of us do know it, but there are a lot of people who, because of selfish gratification (the flesh), don't care. They are focused on the moment and not the consequence of the action.

The word "promiscuity" means to have different sex partners. The Bible teaches us of a powerful spiritual law that comes into effect when two people indulge in a sexual intercourse.

> Don't you realize that the person who unites himself with a prostitute (male or female) becomes [one body] with her (or him)? God says, "The two will be one" (1 Cor. 6:17 God's Word emphasis mine).

The phrase "becomes one body with her" implies that this union will result in what's called soul-ties and in most cases the passing of spirits. A soul-tie is a spiritual merging to another person through the gateway of your body during sexual intercourse. Out of ignorance or unawareness, your soul becomes spiritually connected to the other personality. A person's soul consists of his or her mind, will, and emotions. We've already briefly learned in a previous chapter that the spirit and soul has to have a body to dwell in. When people (male or female) choose a lifestyle that's not consistent with spiritual integrity, it makes them vulnerable for unclean (evil) spirits. Unclean spirits will oppress them and in a good number of cases, posses them. One of the ways evil spirits are passed on to others is through the act of a spiritually illicit sexual intercourse. The human body is a type of gateway for these celestial creatures to travel.

So basically a soul-tie is described as a spiritual connection between one soul and that of another person. This can be godly (as in a God-ordained marriage) or demonic (activity that's not consistent with God's design and purpose). Although some teachings make reference to emotional soul-ties and soul ties developed through "unhealthy" fantasy, the emphasis is generally on those formed through sexual activity. The belief here is that any ungodly sex—that is, any sexual activity that takes place outside of a God-ordained marriage—results in the forming of a spiritually unhealthy soul-tie (an unclean relationship) between the two people with the inclusion of demonism. If either person is not already demonized, this type of relationship is a tool that demons use to gain entry into his or her life, eventually causing havoc and destruction (John 10:10a). The presence of an unclean soul-tie allows the demons from one person to pass to the person he or she is united to. These demons have passed through previous generations, causing a continual perpetuation of this problem and other issues (a curse). Included in the process is the ongoing addition of demons from any other soul-ties (illicit sexual intercourse) that the family ancestor may have had in the past. Ultimately there could be thousands of demons oppressing and emanating through one person. Let's take a closer look at how dangerous this can be.

> When wisdom entereth into thine heart and knowledge
> is pleasant unto thy soul; Discretion shall preserve thee,
> understanding shall keep thee (Prov. 2:10, 11 KJV).

The Holy Bible gives me, you, and anyone else the wisdom of life to live by. This is where everyone can get the wisdom to warn them of life's devastating dangers as well as how to enjoy its purpose. One purpose is:

> To deliver thee from the strange woman (or evil man),
> even from the stranger which flattereth with her words;

> Which forsaketh the guide of her youth, and forgetteth the covenant (relationship) of her God.
>
> For her (or his) house (body) inclineth unto death, and her paths unto the dead.
>
> *None that go unto her* (engages in sexual intercourse) *return again, neither take they hold of the paths of life* (Prov. 2:10–11; 16–19 KJV, emphasis mine).

Without repentance in this matter, it is impossible for any person to get on track with his or her purpose and destiny in life because he or she is out of spiritual position when living a lifestyle of promiscuity.

Evil spirits do not run alone. They run in what are called legions. A legion is an ancient Roman military word that means a large unit of around three to six thousand soldiers. So if there just happens to be one person who is demonically oppressed or possessed, there are thousands of demonic spirits behind the scene coercing that one person; and if this person is possessed, this means that numerous demons are living inside of that human body all at the same time, driving him or her to an early grave. And one avenue these demons are passed on through is sex. Unless that person has a divine encounter with Jesus, he or she will never experience contentment, peace, purpose, or his or her true destiny in life.[1]

Another effect of the curse is in certain areas of illness. This is not to say that all sickness is a result of a person's spiritual condition (the curse). All decay and destruction, which includes sickness, established their roots in the original curse when Adam and Eve disobeyed God. Today's illnesses are an indirect result of the primary curse. So we're not talking about the sickness and disease that are a consequence of the decay process from when God warned them not to eat from the forbidden tree. That is an effect of the curse, but we're talking about an illness that comes from not acknowledging or giving reverence to Him; from ignoring a godly lifestyle. This curse is from a life that has someone or something else as its god; the angle of the curse that comes from willfully ignoring God and His Word.

> Obey the LORD your God, and faithfully follow all his commands and laws that I am giving you today. If you don't, all these [curses] will come to you and stay close to you...

---

1   Luke 8:26-36 (KJV)

The Lord will send [disease after disease] on you, till you have been cut off by death from the land to which you are going (meaning your divine inheritance in this life and eternity). The Lord will send wasting disease, and burning pain, and flaming heat against you…

Jehovah doth smite thee with the ulcer of Egypt, and with emerods, and with scurvy, and with itch, of which thou art not able to be healed (Deut 28:15, GW, Deut 28:21–22, BBE, Deut 28:27, YLT emphasis mine).

Do you often wonder about those diseases we do not have a cure for? According to these passages of Scripture, we learn that incurable diseases come as an effect of a curse. One that comes to mind is AIDS. Statistics tells us that 13.6 percent of the American population is black (www.infoplease.com). That's not a large portion compared to the other inhabitants.

- However, the numbers from the Centers for Disease Control and Prevention state that In 2006, black men accounted for two-thirds of new infections (65%) among all blacks. The rate of new HIV infection for black men was 6 times as high as that of white men, nearly 3 times that of Hispanic/Latino men, and twice that of black women. Also in 2006, the rate of new HIV infection for black women was nearly 15 times as high as that of white women and nearly 4 times that of Hispanic/Latina women.[2]

This gets me wound up and a bit emotional because this disease is not prejudiced. It does not go around saying, "There's a black person, let's infect him or her." So the question is: "What's the problem, and why are African Americans like this?" According to these passages of Scripture, could it be that a large portion of black Americans are out of intimacy and an active relationship with the true God and are experiencing the effect of the curse? Can this be the real issue, the real source behind this taunting trauma? We've just seen that one of the ways that unclean spirits are passed on or transmitted to another person is through spiritually illicit sexual intercourse. Of course, someone can also become infected with this disease by the intravenous use of illegal drugs from a contaminated needle, but the emphasis here is on sex. According to www.blackwomanshealth.

---

2   http://www.cdc.gov/hiv/topics/aa/index.htm

com and other reports, African American communities are being ravaged and attacked by an epidemic of AIDS and other sexually transmitted diseases (STDs).

If AIDS is one of these many demons that are transmitted through soul-ties from sexual intercourse, it is no wonder that there is no material medical cure for it. That's because it's impossible to give a spirit (demon) a physical substance (medicine), seeing that demons are spirits, that they are an invisible reality. This is not to say that all people who are infected with this disease are demon possessed or cursed, because all are not. But it is to say that the celestial creature that carries it has been around and left the effect of the curse as a trail of his presence. Once again, I want to say that we do know that this disease is also transmitted through intravenous drug use with someone who is already infected as well.

Gangs and Violence

Another effect of the curse that's affecting several of our young people comes in the wicked art of gang activity. In the streets it's known as gang banging. Their actions not only include beating people into disability, bad health, and death, which is how banging is defined, but drug dealing, prostitution rings, and everything in between.

There is a God-given desire in every person to be loved and accepted. Only God can fill this emotional appetite. He created this cavity in the human soul as a dwelling place for Himself. When people do not allow God into their heart, for whatever reason, they will fill the desire to be loved and accepted with another person, place, thing, or activity. This violates the first of the Ten Commandments: "Thou shalt have no other gods before me." As we have learned thus far, if the reality of God is ignored in people's lives, they have no power over the curse that has been established at the beginning of time. They will inevitably fill their heart with something or someone else. So a lot of young people look to meet the contentment to be loved and accepted in their peers of the street. Therefore, a pact and a bond (customary trust) are made with others through covenant initiation with a spiritually blind mob that's mostly criminals, or soon will be. This deceptive trust compounds the curse in two ways. The first comes when a person denies God as his or her master, and the other is when someone's total faith is in another person and not God.

> Thus saith the LORD; [Cursed] be the man that trusteth in man, and maketh flesh his arm, and whose heart departeth from the LORD (Jer. 17:5 KJV).

These people bring the curse on themselves and in their subconscious search for the meaning of life become frustrated and attempt to gratify life's reality and meaning in violence.

> What causes fights and quarrels among you? Aren't they caused by the selfish desires that fight to control you? You want what you don't have, so you commit murder. You're determined to have things, but you can't get what you want. You quarrel and fight. You don't have the things you want, because you don't pray for them. When you pray for things, you don't get them because you want them for the wrong reason—for your own pleasure. You unfaithful people! Don't you know that love for this [evil] world is hatred toward God? Whoever wants to be a friend of this world is an enemy of God (James 4:1–4 God's Word).

According to the 2009 National Gang Threat Assessment released by the National Gang Intelligence Center (NGIC) and the National Drug Intelligence Center (NDIC), approximately one million gang members belonging to more than twenty thousand gangs were criminally active in the United States as of September 2008. The assessment was developed through analysis of available federal, state, and local law enforcement information; 2008 NDIC National Drug Threat Survey (NDTS) data; and verified open source information.

"Gangs have long posed a threat to public safety, but as this study shows, gang activity is no longer merely a problem for urban areas. Gang members are increasingly moving to suburban America, bringing with them the potential for increased crime and violence," said Assistant Director Kenneth W. Kaiser, FBI Criminal Investigative Division.

Other key findings are as follows:

- Local street gangs, or neighborhood-based street gangs, remain a significant threat because they still constitute the largest number of gangs nationwide. Most engage in violence in conjunction with a variety of crimes, including retail-level drug distribution.

- According to NDTS data, 58 percent of state and local law enforcement agencies reported that criminal gangs were active in their jurisdictions in 2008 compared with 45 percent of state and local agencies.

- Gang members are migrating from urban to suburban and rural areas, expanding the gangs' influence in most regions. They are doing so for a variety of reasons, including expanding drug distribution territories, increasing illicit revenue, recruiting new members, hiding from law enforcement, and escaping from other gangs. Many suburban and rural communities are experiencing increasing gang-related crime and violence because of expanding gang influence.

- Criminal gangs commit as much as 80 percent of the crime in many communities, according to law enforcement officials throughout the nation. Typical gang-related crimes include alien smuggling, armed robbery, assault, auto theft, drug trafficking, extortion, fraud, home invasions, identity theft, murder, and weapons trafficking.

- Gang members are the primary retail-level distributors of most illicit drugs. They also are increasingly distributing wholesale-level quantities of marijuana and cocaine in most urban and suburban communities.

- Some gangs are trafficking illicit drugs at the regional and national levels; several are capable of competing with United States–based Mexican drug trafficking organizations.

- United States–based gang members illegally cross the United States–Mexico border for the express purpose of smuggling illicit drugs and illegal aliens from Mexico into the United States.

- Many gangs actively use the Internet to recruit new members and to communicate with members in other areas of the United States and in foreign countries.

- Street gangs and outlaw motorcycle gangs pose a growing threat to law enforcement along the United States–Canada border. They frequently associate with Canada-based gangs and criminal organizations to facilitate various criminal activities, including drug smuggling into the United States.

- Some of the most irrational and tragic crimes in America are committed through the gang epidemic in this country.[3]

The Louisiana weekly reported that In his 2006 book, *The Audacity of Hope*, Barack Obama wrote, "I also believe that when a gangbanger shoots indiscriminately into a crowd because he feels someone disrespected him, we have a problem of morality ... we need to acknowledge that there's a hole in his heart, one that government programs alone may not be able to repair."[4]

The Other Side

Another angle of the curse to consider is on the other side of the continuum, which is camouflaged in politics and business. It's called white-collar crime. The Gospels teach us that when Jesus was led out into the wilderness to be tempted for us by the devil (Hebrews 4:15), the devil wanted to be worshiped by Him.

> Once more the Devil took Him (Jesus) to a high mountain and showed Him all the *kingdoms of the world* and their glory. The Devil said to Him, *"I will give you this if you bow down and worship me"* (Matt. 4:8–9 God's Word emphasis mine).

This same spiritual principle and technique of the enemy is at work today. Satan is dominating people in authoritative positions whose desire is to run the world out of selfish ambition, not in willful submission to God. History has also proven this, from the Tower of Babel to Adolph Hitler and a few other up-to-date dictators. Most of these people are deceived by

---

3   The following agencies contributed to the report: the Bureau of Alcohol, Tobacco, Firearms and Explosives; Department of Justice, Bureau of Justice Assistance; Department of Justice, Bureau of Justice Statistics; Department of Justice, Organized Crime Drug Enforcement Task Force; Drug Enforcement Administration; Federal Bureau of Investigation; Federal Bureau of Prisons; National Drug Intelligence Center; National Gang Intelligence Center; Office of National Drug Control Policy, High Intensity Drug Trafficking Areas; United States Army Criminal Investigations Division; United States Customs and Border Protection; United States Immigration and Customs Enforcement; United States Marshals Service; numerous state and local law enforcement agencies; and the Canada Border Service Agency.

4   http://www.louisianaweekly.com/news.php?viewStory=1621
Audacity of Hope, Barack Obama, Crown/Three Rivers Press, October, 17th 2006.

the adrenaline of power and the deceptive comfort of money and material possessions. They will illegally do what they think needs to be done to keep themselves, their peers, and their allies in position. But all at the same time, they are victims of the curse and pawns of the devil.

White-collar crimes are fraud, bribery, insider trading, embezzlement, computer crime, medical crime, public corruption, identity theft, environmental crime, RICO crimes, occupational crime, financial fraud, forgery, and human trafficking (the selling of people). The tool of the trade is paperwork, the computer, and in several cases a network of organized wrongdoing. White-collar crimes go largely undetected and consist of business and political entities. *I'm not saying that all business and political entities are corrupt, because they're not, and you and I both should know this, but there are a large number of people who are not honest businessmen and women in their career. They're corrupt.*

On this end of the continuum of the curse are the ones that the principalities of the power of darkness (demons) are using to gain and maintain control of this world.[5] One element of the area of this is the cocaine epidemic in America that's a result of wholesale distribution. We know about the drug problem in the low-income districts throughout this country. But the question is, "How does the cocaine get there?" These people, who can't find jobs, are homeless, are on welfare and food stamps, and are victims of drug addiction (another effect of the curse) can't afford to go to Bogotá, Columbia, and smuggle the vast amount of cocaine into this country that's sold across America on a daily basis. Look at this news article that was stamped for immediate release on November 15, 2007, by the FBI to the public.

SEVEN FORMER PUBLIC OFFICIALS SENTENCED FOR PARTICIPATING IN BRIBERY AND EXTORTION CONSPIRACY

WASHINGTON—Seven former public officials were sentenced this week in the U.S. District Court for the District of Arizona, in Tucson, for their roles in a widespread bribery and extortion conspiracy, Assistant Attorney General Alice S. Fisher of the Criminal Division announced today.

The charges arise from Operation Lively Green, an undercover investigation conducted by the Federal Bureau

---

5   Ephesians 6:12.

of Investigation (FBI) that began in December 2001. Forty-five additional defendants have been sentenced and four others have pleaded guilty and await sentencing.

The defendants had each pleaded guilty to one count of conspiring to enrich themselves by obtaining cash bribes from persons they believed to be narcotics traffickers, who were actually FBI agents, in return for their assistance, protection, and participation in the activities of an illegal narcotics trafficking organization that distributed cocaine from Arizona to other locations in the southwestern United States. *In order to protect the shipments of cocaine, the defendants wore official uniforms, carried official forms of identification and used official vehicles, when necessary, to prevent police stops, searches and seizures of the narcotics as they drove the cocaine shipments through checkpoints manned by the U.S. Border Patrol, the Arizona Department of Public Safety and Nevada law enforcement officers.*[6]

These types of public officials, as well as whoever practices corrupt business deals, are the people who the book of Revelations refer to as the kings and merchants of the earth who commit fornication with the whore that rides the beast.

For all nations have drunk (participated) of the wine of the wrath (dominated outrage) of her fornication (intimate wickedness), and the kings of the earth (*corrupt politicians*) have committed fornication with her, and the merchants of the earth (*corrupt businesspeople*) are waxed [rich] through the abundance of her delicacies (activity and lifestyle) (Rev. 18:3 KJV emphasis mine).

Because of the effect of the curse, the spiritual blindness of people will cause them not to understand or even realize that they are participants in Satan's kingdom. This "whore" that is spoken about in the book of Revelation is a powerful demonic spirit that coerces the minds and thoughts of people, especially the unsaved, including those that are in authoritative

---

6   http://phoenix.fbi.gov/dojpressrel/2007/ph111507.htm

positions throughout the world. Its purpose is to use people to carry out the devils will on earth as in Matthew 4:8–9:

> ... Fall down and worship me and I'll give you the kingdoms of the world.

The reason the Scripture explains an illegal lifestyle is like having intercourse with a whore is because of the emotional gratification that a person or organism experiences when the appetites of selfishness, lust, power, pride, and greed are fed. It parallels the inner-soul contentment of having sexual intercourse. Usually this emotion comes prior to, during, and upon completion of the ungodly action or desired goal. It is a type of counterfeit that resembles godly contentment. As I've already mentioned, this curse of the spiritual whore is also spoken about in the book of Zechariah. Its foundation lies in mental confusion, which is what the word Shinar (Hebrew for Babylon) means. Listen to what the angel of God says to the prophet Zechariah:

> I looked up again and saw a flying scroll. The angel asked me, "What do you see?" "I see a flying scroll," I answered. "It's 30 feet long and 15 feet wide." Then he said to me, "This is a [curse] that will *go out all over the earth*. The one side of the scroll says that every thief will be forced away (from God). The other side of the scroll says that everyone who takes an oath will be forced away. I will send out a [curse], declares the LORD of Armies, and *it will enter the houses of thieves and the houses of those who take oaths in my name*. It will stay in their houses and destroy the timber and stone" (Zech. 5:1–4 God's Word emphasis mine).

According to these Scriptures, one of the possible reasons a family deteriorates and there may be major emotional dysfunctions could be as a result of someone living an ungodly lifestyle. The curse does not only rest in the structure of the building but signifies that the word "houses" includes a person's direct family and family members. The one who bought the curse into the house can be the cause of it, continuing from generation to generation. Just think about how many families may be living in a house that's cursed and they don't even realize it. All they know is that there are a ton of problems and extraordinary inconsistencies in that home.

The wickedness of ancient Babylon that existed during Old Testament times has come to symbolize the spiritual city of evil in this time of the New Testament church in which we currently live.[7] As a result of the curse, anyone who chooses not to become a born-again believer in Jesus Christ falls under one of these three categories and is a citizen of Babylon, some willfully and some out of ignorance.

They are:

a) Corrupt politicians or businesspersons
b) Anyone who's a participant in any religion other than the Gospel of Jesus Christ
c) And all who refuse to acknowledge that Jesus is Lord and the Son of God.

Jesus Christ Himself said:

> Anyone who isn't with me opposes me, and anyone who isn't working with me is actually working against me (Matt. 12:30 NLT).

---

7   Revelation 18:1–2 (KJV).

To him that overcometh will I grant to sit with me in my throne, even as I also overcame, and am set down with my Father in his throne. He that hath an ear, let him hear what the Spirit saith unto the churches. Rev. 3:21-22 (KJV)

CHAPTER FOUR

A REAL-LIFE ISSUE

Let's take a closer look at the previous three categories that make up the spiritual city of Babylon. The Bible speaks about this spiritual city in the book of Revelation.

> Then another angel followed him through the skies, saying, "Babylon is fallen, is fallen—that *great city*—because she seduced the nations of the world and made them share the wine of her intense impurity and sin" (Rev. 14:8 TLB).

The first of the three categories is the corrupt political and business practices in our nation as well as the world. We've already touched bases in the preceding chapter on one element of corruption by certain public officials in the illegal craft of drug trafficking. *Also keep in mind that I'm not advocating that all politics or businesspeople are corrupt, because they're not.* But because of the negative spiritual domino effect of the curse upon a person's intellectual and emotional being, any and all people are vulnerable and can become victims of this deceptive trauma. As a result, the effect of the curse is carried over into a person's family, career, livelihood, and nation no matter who they are if they refuse to take it upon themselves to correct this crisis according to God's standards.

Merriam Webster's Dictionary defines the word city as, "An inhabited place of greater size, population, or importance than a town or village."

This city (Babylon) *is not a physical location but a spiritual condition. And the spiritual condition of a person makes this physical world we live in the field where spiritual activities are carried out.*

It is spiritual in the sense that our thoughts and emotions are invisible, but because of the volatile activity of our thoughts and fluctuation of our emotions, we know they are real. Everyone knows that their thoughts and emotions are real, yet we can't taste, touch, or smell them because they are invisible. This invisible activity is confirmation that they are spiritual. There is a spiritual world where celestial beings dwell, and the intrinsic function of the human spirit and soul is receptive to this spiritual realm. All people are spiritual, whether they realize it or not.

> So God created man in his *own* image, in the image of God created he him; male and female created he them (Gen. 1:27 KJV).

We all are created by God and fashioned in His image or *spirit,* **but we're not all God's family.**

The human conscience is the voice of our spirit. But our mind, emotions, and desires are a function of our soul, and both of these entities are spiritual (invisible). Most people think they can manage life without an active relationship with God, who is ultimate Spirit (John 4:25). But the truth is that it's impossible to do that.

> Now therefore hearken unto me, O ye children: for blessed *are they that* keep my ways. Hear instruction, and be wise, and refuse it not. Blessed *is* the man that heareth me, watching daily at my gates, waiting at the posts of my doors. For whoso findeth me findeth life, and shall obtain favour of the LORD. *But he that sinneth against me wrongeth his own soul: all they that hate me love death* (Prov. 8:32–36 emphasis mine).

That's what makes a person a citizen of Babylon, living a life without an intimate relationship with God. Basically, the majority of the people in the world who deny the true God live in this corrupt spiritual city because of their *mindset.* There is a wise saying that says, "*The mind attracts its own and nothing comes to it that does not belong to it.*" As a consequence of the effect of the curse, there are people whose lives are powerless over lust, money, greed, and selfishness. Not understanding this spiritual law of the mind causes them to unknowingly draw other people with the same characteristics into their inner circle of survival. The biblical name of this spiritual condition is the city of Babylon, which means confusion. In other words, Babylon's citizens are people without a relationship with God and are ignorantly confused about authentic life. Nearly every one of them is dishonest, selfish, greedy of heart, and rebellious against God. In addition to this, those who are extremely violent live there too.

One of the major sources of this city is a powerful evil spirit that's metaphorically portrayed as a whorish woman (Rev. 17:5). This evil spirit coerces corrupt activity in the human race. The term "whorish" is used because she seeks to take the intimate place in our heart that belongs to God. *The inner gratification that is satisfied from the thrill of interacting in a corrupt lifestyle is a counterfeit spiritual intimacy.* A lifestyle of integrity toward God is how and why we were created to live. In other words, this is how a person has a spiritual intercourse with an evil spirit. The opposite of intimacy with God results in emotional activity with a morally wrong lifestyle. It is similar to the inner emotion of the heart when reaching a physical climax during a sexual intercourse. It's a type of activity that makes your adrenaline flow, especially when you think that no one knows it but you and you prosperously came out on top. So the spiritual term whore is also used because it denotes a life that is not being intimately lived out in relation to Almighty God. We were created to have a spiritually intimate relationship with God. Life without this relationship is classified by God as spiritual whoredom.

> And the person who turneth unto those having [familiar spirits], and unto the wizards, *to go a whoring after them*, I have even set My face against that person, and cut him off from the midst of his people (Lev. 20:6 YLT emphasis mine).

Because God created humans to subdue and manage the earth, people are wired to be in charge, with the desire to run something. But as I've just said, without an active, intimate relationship with Him, it's impossible to do and reap the desired effects that were initially established for the human race. Therefore, people will do what they think needs to be done, how they think it should be done, by any means possible, to keep themselves and their team in the driver's seat. And the most prominent place of authority is in the business and political arena.

> Shall the throne of iniquity have fellowship with thee, which frameth mischief by a law? They gather themselves

together against the soul of the righteous, and condemn the innocent blood … (Ps. 94:20 KJV).

What causes fights and quarrels among you? Aren't they caused by the selfish desires that fight to control you? You want what you don't have, so you commit murder. You're determined to have things, but you can't get what you want. You quarrel and fight. You don't have the things you want, because you don't pray for them. When you pray for things, you don't get them because you want them for the wrong reason—for your own pleasure. You unfaithful people! Don't you know that love for this {evil} world is hatred toward God? Whoever wants to be a friend of this world is an enemy of God (James 4:1–4 God's Word).

False Religion

The second part of the spiritual city Babylon consists of anyone who participates in a religion that's not the Gospel of Jesus Christ.

First we must ask the question, "What defines a religion as false?" There are so many other beliefs in the world, how do we determine which is true and which is false, and if there is such a thing as a "false religion"? There are various religions that have creation myths describing the origins of the universe, and through them, the meaning of life, the underlying order of nature, and destiny of humans and the cosmos.

This reality of God has been a mystery to some people since the beginning of the world. But the true God has always made Himself known to people He has chosen to reveal Himself through to the world. Not only has He made Himself known through these people to the world, but He has backed up what He told them to proclaim with supernatural acts.

For the [*invisible*] things of him (God) from the creation of the world are [*clearly seen*], being understood by the things that are made, *even* his eternal power and Godhead; so that they (*whoever doubt the true God's existence*) are without excuse (Rom. 1:20 KJV, emphasis mine).

The apostle Paul, who is one of the several persons in history who the true God revealed Himself to with the purpose of informing the world of

His Son, is the author of the book of Romans in the Bible. In the previous verses leading up to verse 20 in chapter one, he boldly states his calling.

> Paul, a servant of Jesus Christ, [called] *to be* an apostle, separated unto the gospel (good news) of God, (Which he had promised afore by his prophets in the holy Scriptures,) Concerning his Son Jesus Christ our Lord, which was made of the seed of David according to the flesh; And declared *to be* the Son of God with power, according to the spirit of holiness, by the resurrection from the dead (Rom. 1:1–4 KJV, emphasis mine).

After Paul tells us of his calling and purpose, he goes on to proclaim how the true God has made known His judgments against the human race for morally wrong lifestyles that were lived out in history.

> For the wrath (anger that results in justice) of God is revealed from heaven against all ungodliness and unrighteousness of men, who hold the truth (they who know God exist) in unrighteousness (but don't live like it) Because that which may be known of God is manifest in them; for God hath showed *it* unto them (Rom. 1:18–19, KJV emphasis mine).

The true God has actually showed Himself to the world on several occasions. But because He loves us so much, He created the human race with a mind to think for ourselves; a mind with freedom of choice. As a result of this intellectual freedom, people have chosen not to believe who He has revealed and proclaimed Himself to be through creation and/or the people He has chosen to work through, as well as the supernatural interaction with the human race through history.

Historical records in most all cultures declare the destruction of the world by water thousands of years ago. Despite the historical similarities of the flood, the story has a unique Hebraic perspective (for those of you who are not biblical students, the Hebrews are a race of people the true God chose to reveal Himself through to the world centuries ago).

The story of the flood from these other cultures was claimed to be mainly a result of the disagreement of the idol gods.[1] Idols in that dispensation of time and even in some modern-day cultures today were made of wood,

---

1   *Encyclopedia Britannica 2008 Ultimate Reference* (encyclopedia articles 121 Noah) [biblical figure].

some were made of stone, and others were made of jewels or some type of artifacts. Some people even honored celestial bodies, such as the moon, stars, and the sun. These objects that are only material substances were worshiped as God and have no life or power in them period. But in the book of Genesis the flood resulted from the moral corruption of humanity sanctioned by God through a man named Noah.

This same God has proven Himself to be authentic down through the corridors of time by the many supernatural acts of confirmation; from the creation of the universe to the parting of the Red Sea and the providing for a whole nation for forty years in the desert.

The survival of Noah and his family through the worldwide flood that destroyed the earth and everything in it is affirmation of the omnipotence and benevolence of the one, true, righteous God. Following their survival, Noah and his family were commanded to undertake the renewal of history that has brought us where we are today (Gen. 9:1–18).

With the replenishing and renewal process of humanity that was commanded to Noah and his sons came one of the most provocative supernatural acts the world has ever heard of. This was the birth, life, crucifixion, and resurrection of the Messiah. This further proves His sovereignty as well as His proclamation of being the one and only true God when He raised Jesus Christ from the dead.

Since the beginning of creation, God has always worked through people who will submit to him. By His Holy Spirit through the apostle John, this same God that has proven to be the only true God by His supernatural acts through history has commanded the world to believe on Jesus Christ.

> And this is his *commandment* that we should believe on the name of his Son Jesus Christ, and love one another, as he gave us commandment (1 John 3:23 KJV emphasis mine).

So the original question was, "What defines a religion as false?" The Holy Spirit of God through the same apostle John gives us the answer.

> Every spirit that confesseth that Jesus Christ is come in the flesh is of God: *And every spirit that confesseth not that Jesus Christ is come in the flesh is not of God: and this is that spirit of antichrist, whereof ye have heard that it should come;*

and even now already is it in the world (1 John 4:2–3 KJV, emphasis mine).

So to sum up this worldwide debate about the true God who has unequivocally proven Himself down through the corridors of time to be authentic to the human race has stated in the Bible by His Holy Spirit that any person, family, city or nation that denies the gospel of Jesus Christ is honoring a false religion.

Refusing the Truth

The third category of residents that populate the spiritual city Babylon includes those who are not practicing any religious beliefs at all; especially the people who say no to acknowledging that Jesus Christ is Lord of all the earth; those who refuse to acknowledge the truth and to retain God in their thinking. Remember that God loved the human race enough that He gave us freedom of choice, the ability to think for ourselves. When someone continues to ignore the truth about God, He will not force them to change their mind. He will allow them to keep living life in the state of mind they have chosen because they willfully put forth the effort to continue to ignore His obvious revealing.

> Since they didn't bother to acknowledge God, God quit bothering them and let them run loose.
>
> And then all hell broke loose: rampant evil, grabbing and grasping, vicious backstabbing.
>
> They made life hell on earth with their envy, wanton killing, bickering, and cheating. Look at them: mean-spirited, venomous, fork-tongued God-bashers.
>
> Bullies, swaggerers, insufferable windbags! *They keep inventing new ways of wrecking lives.*
>
> They ditch their parents when they get in the way. Stupid, slimy, cruel, cold-blooded.
>
> And it's not as if they don't know better. They know perfectly well they're spitting in God's face.
>
> And they don't care—worse, *they hand out prizes to those who do the worst things best!* (Romans 1:28–32 TM, emphasis mine).

When a person seeks to live life according to their own dictates and not according to God's standards the bible teaches us that this is the same character of Satan (Isaiah14:12-15). God created Adam & Eve on the sixth day of creation in his image; a spirit within a soul, and placed this essence in a body. And then God rested on the seventh day from all his works. The number seven is symbolic of completion. So to live in harmony with God's provisions (the gift of salvation) makes us complete (requirements met for an intimate relationship with God) in Jesus Christ. Jesus is the completion of God's salvation plan for humanity. If a person is not in Christ they are not spiritually complete and are still operating in a secular capacity. Remember, the spiritual authority was lost through disobedience which caused them to rely on the resources of human attributes and not divine relationship. These human resources were given to them on the sixth day; the day they were created and received. The sixth day indicates the human spirit created on the sixth day, the soul on the sixth day, and the body on the sixth day: 666.

In the book of Revelation the scriptures tell us that the number 666 is a number of a man.

> Here is wisdom. Let him that hath understanding count the number of the beast: for it is the number of a man; and his number is Six hundred threescore *and* six. Rev 13:18 (KJV)

These passages are spiritually definitive in that it describes the beast that is destroying society as earthly nations (men & women) who have been in power and are currently in power whose focus was on and is still on running the world and not serving Almighty God. In other words living life without Christ is like living life as a beast (wild animal) including having the personality of Satan and his demons.

> Be not thou afraid when one is made rich, when the glory of his house is increased; For when he dieth he shall carry nothing away: his glory shall not descend after him. Though while he lived he blessed his soul: and *men* will praise thee, when thou doest well to thyself. He shall go to the generation of his fathers; they shall never see light. Man *that is* in honour (highly respected), and understandeth not (life without God), is like the *beasts that* perish. Psalms 49:16-20 (KJV emphasis mine)

I say Satan's personality because when a person manages their life ignoring God and are focused on self, material possessions, pride, and power they have put themselves in the place that belongs to God (Ezekiel 28:1-19).

The psychological state that results from ignoring God is a spiritual position that makes a person victim to the curse. *A person's mentality shows in his or her morality.* Have you ever known a person who keeps doing the same thing over and over and over and can't seem to break loose from it? It seems as though he or she is *stuck!*

> The wicked man (or woman) is doomed by his own sins; they are [*ropes*] that catch and [*hold him*]. He (or she) shall die because he will not [*listen to the truth*]; he has let himself be led away into incredible folly (Prov. 5:22–23 TLB, emphasis mine).

Merriam Webster's Dictionary and Thesaurus defines the word "folly" in this verse as:

a: criminally or tragically foolish actions or conduct.
b: *obs: evil wickedness* ; *esp:* lewd behavior

This verse explains that by not "*listening to the truth,*" countless people are trapped into an assortment of life's foolishnesses and can't break away. The mentality of ignoring the truth about God is a derivative of an ill spiritual condition that's the fruit of a wounded soul. There are also other types of inflictions that cause a soul to be wounded too, but the major one is life without the true God.

But God shall [wound] the head of his enemies, *and* the hairy scalp of such an one as goeth on still in his trespasses (Ps. 68:21 KJV emphasis mine).

CHAPTER FIVE

ARE YOU WOUNDED?

Merriam Webster's Dictionary and Thesaurus states a wound as follows:

> **1:** an injury to the body (as from violence, accident, or surgery) that typically involves laceration or breaking of a membrane (as the skin) and usually damage to underlying tissues.

> **2:** a mental or emotional hurt or blow.

Many of you have seen the ugly appearance of physical wounds in one form or another, whether it was from a small incident, serious automobile accident, an act of violence, a crime, or a physical illness, etc. These injuries have to be attended to with medical care, or they may result in becoming infected.

There are some wounds that are infected and just fester with contaminating bacteria that oozes around and through the bandage. The infection can get so bad that the infected limb in some cases has to be amputated if serious care is not applied.

Now let's compare this illustration to the second definition of the wound, which *is a mental or emotional hurt or blow*

First of all, every person is born into this world spiritually wounded at birth. That's because we come into this world separated from God as a result of the first human beings' act of defiance (see Gen. 2:16–17).

In the process of physical growth starting at birth through young adulthood (and for some even after adulthood), people at various points in life's journey will emotionally venture out to find the meaning, purpose, and contentment of life. Some will do this knowingly and some people do this subconsciously, but the point is that this quest of purpose is actually a spiritual desire for relationship with God. Everyone does eventually have this longing, but all do not pursue it in its proper perspective. Some don't pursue it at all; they just go through life hurt. When the longing starts, it is a lifelong craving unless the heart is filled with God. If not, there's emptiness coupled with a feeling of isolation, loneliness, and lack of purpose until a person goes to his or her grave. There are a lot of people whose hearts are filled with everything but God. We come into this world wounded (separated from God) but unwittingly have a desire for God. He has put this innate yearning in each person, and He is the only one who can *fill it!* Without an active, intimate relationship with Him, people will go through life emotionally wounded. If this wound goes unhealed, its continuous festering is the foundation for several other wounds that cause trauma in the person's life and everyone he or she comes into contact with, including family.

Piggy-backed on top of the God wound are other types of wounds that happen in different ways and in different seasons and from diverse sources in a person's life. A lot of people harbor multiple wounds. Other than the inherited injury from being born into this world separated from God, a person can incur a wound or wounds from four additional areas. They are:

Childhood Wounds. Such wounds are caused by our parents and primary caregivers. These are usually the deepest and most painful of the wounds we have. Some can be severe wounds resulting from the trauma of sexual abuse and severe physical abuse. More typically, they come from the experiences of parental fighting and divorce. When parents do not take the time to listen, understand, and empathize with their children, they inflict such wounds.

Relationship Wounds. Such wounds are caused by the painful actions, words, and events of your current/previous relationships. Negative memories of past failed relationships inflict relationship wounds. Painful experiences of toxic and abusive behaviors and actions by you or current and former partners also originate with them.

Self-Inflicted Wounds. Such wounds are self-inflicted because of decisions, behaviors, and actions. Serious wounds can occur from alcohol and drug abuse. Similarly, errors in judgment may have led you to make other bad choices in life—in relationships, careers, and finances.

Other Wounds. Such wounds are caused by siblings, school, friends, work, relatives, and society. They are caused by factors like excessive teasing in school over a period of time, an abusive uncle calling you "fat" every time he sees you, or a boss reinforcing your beliefs that you are not smart enough or good enough.

All of these wounds not only cause emotional pain but also stress, fear, bad habits, and addiction, which result in serious problems because of the effectiveness of the spiritual curse. The primary domain of the curse is in the atmosphere and a life of unhealed wounds can cause a person to experience its effect. And then there's the spiritual curses that are implemented by people who are willfully interacting with demonism (satanic worship, witchcraft, black magic, voodoo, etc.), which compounds the frustration of the victim as well as in keeping him or her stuck in a certain lifestyle.

Emotional Wounds Can Create Scars for Life

There are also wounds that are a result of other traumatic experiences. These emotional wounds come from being a victim of a violent crime such as rape, robbery, kidnapping, murder of a loved one, etc. These crimes are committed by people who have unsettled implications from the four areas of wounds that are stated above that were never healed. However, all wounds can have a lifelong scar if not cared for.

Unless attended to, emotional wounds can have a devastating affect on a person's life. Yes, they can possibly be a lifelong injury of frustration, annoyance, and disappointment. Have you ever stopped and wondered when you see a homeless person lying on a bus bench, or the ground, or begging for money, "How deep and disturbing is the wound that's demoralizing him or her?" What about a person who just stands and talks to him or herself? Or the person who looks and smells like he or she hasn't bathed in a month or so? The trauma that causes a person to be a victim of unhealed emotional wounds can rob a person of the fulfillment of five basic emotional needs:

Safety: The sense of safety is derived from the belief, "I am safe and my loved ones are safe." Trauma victims constantly worry that something bad will happen to them. That creates a constant state of tension. Likewise, we normally believe that people we love are safe. Trauma victims constantly worry that something bad is going to happen to their loved ones. For example, whenever their spouses or children are late getting back home, they feel sure that something terrible has happened to them.

Trust: Trust is derived from the belief, "I can rely on myself and people around me." Some trauma victims begin to believe, "I can't trust myself because I can't protect myself." They tend to feel suspicious of others' motives and experience constant anxiety in the presence of other people.

Control: Control is derived from the belief, "I control what happens in my life, and I can influence others' behavior toward me." Some trauma victims begin to believe that they have no control over their lives except to try to survive the injuries others may inflict on them.

Esteem: Esteem is derived from the belief, "I am loveable and others, too, are loveable." Having experienced intense hate by a perpetrator during acts of violence destroys that belief in some trauma victims. Self criticism, self-dislike, and even self-hate result from interpersonal trauma.

Intimacy: Some trauma victims are changed forever insofar as never allowing anyone to come emotionally close to them because they can't trust themselves or others.

Certain emotional wounds can be far more crippling than physical injuries.

Hurt People, Hurt People

There is a saying that says, "If a person is not part of the solution, then he or she is part of the problem!" It's true: people who have been hurt wind up hurting others if they don't seek healing. In other words, the victim becomes the villain. Often they inflict the same kind of injury they themselves received. Hurt people are all around us—neighbors, church members, family members, ministry leaders, even ourselves.

The bitterness from certain wounds can cause people to lash out at others. Some can be subtle, while others are just flat-out violent. Because of the God-given desire to be loved and accepted, people with unhealed wounds carry this dysfunction into relationships in their life. There are people who are just associates but act out toward each other in anger. There are people who are considered as friends and act out as well. Then there are relationships of distorted sexual identity where people have coupled together with the same sex. And then there are naturally heterosexual unions too, but the most customary relationship in society is the family.

There are many cases of domestic violence resulting from emotionally wounded people. The word domestic means living near or about human habitation and the things relating to a household or family. Domestic violence is any physical, verbal, sexual, or psychological abuse that people use against a former or current intimate partner. It refers to a number of criminal behaviors, such as assault and battery, sexual assault, stalking, harassment, violation of a civil restraining order, homicide, and other offenses that occur in the course of a domestic violence incident, such as arson, robbery, malicious destruction of property, and endangering a minor. No person can validly consent to a breach of the peace or a battery that may result in serious injury or death.

Many of these victims are women. In the year 2000, the United Nations' study on the status of women stated that every fifteen seconds somewhere in this country a woman is battered, usually by her intimate partner. Nearly 31 percent of women in the United States report being physically or sexually abused by an intimate partner at some point. And we all know from the broadcast of the local and national news that domestic violence as well as public violence has increased since the year of 2000.

Domestic violence also includes child abuse. Child abuse by hurt people who hurt others can be physical, sexual, or emotional maltreatment or neglect of children by parents, guardians, or others responsible for a child's welfare. Physical abuse is characterized by physical injury, usually inflicted as a result of a beating or inappropriately harsh discipline. Sexual abuse includes molestation, incest, rape, prostitution, or use of a child for pornographic purposes. Neglect can be physical in nature (abandonment, failure to seek needed health care), educational (failure to see that a child is attending school), or emotional (abuse of a spouse or another child in the child's presence, allowing a child to witness adult substance abuse). Inappropriate punishment, verbal abuse, and scapegoating are also forms of emotional or psychological child abuse.

Of course, it is a no brainer that violence is a public issue too. Peer group violence, which includes workplace violence, is when crimes are committed in the place of work. One problem case is child abuse by a pediatrician who was charged for molestation of nine little girls and possibly up to one hundred kids over the span of a decade.

A Delaware pediatrician linked to horrific sexual abuse of patients as young as 3 months old assaulted as many as 100 children, investigators believe. The doctor was arrested after a toddler complained to her mom that the doctor had hurt her. Police found videotapes that the pediatrician had filmed of himself assaulting his patients in his gaily decorated examination rooms and a renovated garage next door as their parents were told to wait outside, reports the *News Journal*. The doctor currently faces charges of sexual assault on nine girls, including an infant, but those charges will likely be expanded.

This man was doctor to many children in the small town of Lewes, population 3,000. "It makes me sick," said a parent. "I've worked with little toddlers and babies. I can't imagine anybody hurting any of them." Authorities are basing their estimates of victims on flash drives of video recordings recovered from the doctor's office. "The community is in shock," said a local pastor. "We're praying for everyone affected by this" (*Newser*).[1]

This incident happened in December of 2009, and just imagine the emotional scars that have been embedded into the souls of these kids. Because of the domino effect of hurting people who hurt people, if these wounds are not healed, they too can fester over into the lives of other people who will be in these innocent victims' circle of relationships as they grow up.

Other acts of public violence in the workplace include the several cases where people have returned and assaulted or even murdered coworkers on the job.

- There were 900 homicides, 36,500 sexual assaults, and 70,000 robberies in the workplace on average each year between 1993 and 1999.

- Of the incidents, 1.54 percent were employee against employee; 2.13 percent were employee against supervisor; 3.7 percent were customers against workers.

- Of the incidents, 1.38 percent were attributed to personality conflicts; 2.15 percent were attributed to family problems; 3.10 percent to drug or alcohol abuse; 4.7 percent were nonspecific; and 5.7 percent were attributed to firing or layoff.[2]

---

1   www.newser.com/story/76858/pediatrician-molested-up-to-100-kids-cops.html
2   (http://www.moldmakingtechnology.com/articles/040309.html)

Here is an article that talks about an act of violence that happened in a different workplace on September 17, 2009 by the *Yale Daily News*:

> Law enforcement officials have charged an animal lab technician with the murder of a female Yale graduate student who was strangled to death last week, the *Yale Daily News Reports*.
>
> Police arrested a 24-year-old man this morning at a Super 8 motel in Cromwell, Conn. The young man had been staying there since yesterday morning, when police released him from custody after serving him with two warrants—one to search his Middletown, Conn., apartment and the other to take samples of his DNA...
>
> Someone familiar with the investigation told the *Yale Daily News* yesterday that the young man's DNA matched evidence taken from the Yale research facility where the female student's body was found Sunday, the day she had planned to wed...
>
> As an animal lab technician, the technician is responsible for feeding and watering the animals used for testing in the research lab and for cleaning their cages. New Haven Police Chief... describe the murder as a workplace crime.
>
> "This was not about New Haven crime or university crime or domestic crime," The Police Chief said. "*This was workplace violence.*"

Another circumstance of unhealed wounds is the hurt people who hurt themselves. This is acted out into self-mutilation and/or suicide.

Self-mutilation is a general term for a variety of forms of intentional self-harm without the wish to die. Cutting one's skin with razors or knives is the most common pattern of self-mutilation. Others include biting, hitting, or bruising oneself; picking or pulling at skin or hair; burning oneself with lighted cigarettes; or amputating parts of the body.

Self-mutilation has become a major public health concern as its incidence appears to have risen since the early 1990s. One source estimates that 0.75 percent of the general American population practices self-mutilation. The incidence of self-mutilation is highest among teenage females, patients diagnosed with borderline personality disorder, and patients diagnosed with one of the dissociative disorders. Over half of self-mutilators were sexually abused as children, and many also suffer from eating disorders

The relationship of self-mutilation to suicide is still debated even though statistics show that nearly 50 percent of individuals who injure themselves also attempt suicide at some point in their lives. Many researchers think suicide attempts reflect feelings of rejection or hopelessness, while self-mutilation results from feelings of shame or a need to relieve tension (*Gale Encyclopedia of Medicine*, 3rd ed. 2006).

National Statistics on suicide:

General

- Over 33,000 people in the United States die by suicide every year.

- In 2006 (latest available data), there were 33,300 reported suicide deaths.

- Suicide is the fourth leading cause of death for adults between the ages of eighteen and sixty-five years in the United States, with 27,321 suicides.

- Currently, suicide is the eleventh leading cause of death in the United States.

- A person dies by suicide about every sixteen minutes in the United States. An attempt is estimated to be made once every minute.

- Ninety percent of all people who die by suicide have a diagnosable psychiatric disorder at the time of their death.

- There are four male suicides for every female suicide, but three times as many females as males attempt suicide.

- Every day, approximately ninety Americans take their own life, and 2,300 more attempt to do so.

Youth

- Suicide is the fifth leading cause of death among those five to fourteen years old.

- Suicide is the third leading cause of death among those fifteen to twenty-four years old.

- Between the mid-1950s and the late 1970s, the suicide rate among US males aged fifteen to twenty-four more than tripled (from 6.3 per 100,000 in 1955 to 21.3 in 1977). Among females aged fifteen to twenty-four, the rate more than doubled during this period (from 2.0 to 5.2). The youth suicide rate generally leveled off during the 1980s and early 1990s and since the mid-1990s has been steadily decreasing.

- Among young people aged ten to fourteen years, the rate has doubled in the last two decades.

- Between 1980 and 1996, the suicide rate for African American males aged fifteen to nineteen has also doubled.

- Risk factors for suicide among the young include suicidal thoughts, psychiatric disorders (such as depression, impulsive aggressive behavior, bipolar disorder, and certain anxiety disorders), drug and/or alcohol abuse, and previous suicide attempts, with the risk increased if there is situational stress and access to firearms.

Depression

- Over 60 percent of all people who die by suicide suffer from major depression. If one includes alcoholics who are depressed, this figure rises to over 75 percent.

- Depression affects nearly 10 percent of Americans ages eighteen and over in a given year, or more than 24 million people.

- More Americans suffer from depression than coronary heart disease (17 million), cancer (12 million), and HIV/AIDS (1 million).

- About 15 percent of the population will suffer from clinical depression at some time during their lifetime. Thirty percent of all clinically depressed patients attempt suicide; half of them ultimately die by suicide.

- *Depression is among the most treatable of psychiatric illnesses.* Between 80 percent and 90 percent of people with depression respond positively to treatment, and almost all patients gain some relief from their symptoms. *But first, depression has to be recognized.*[3]

Depression can easily set in a person's emotions when the unhealed wounds are not treated and cared for. All of the maladies that have been discussed in this chapter are a type of infection in society as a result of untreated and uncared for emotional wounds. These actions are the consequence of the spiritual curse's effect that began at the beginning of time and is the continuation of bondage unless taken seriously and dealt with. Yes! These have been, are, and will continue to be passed on from generation to generation until you personally face yours to stop the cycle in your family and relationships. Some people just flat out choose to ignore God, the author of life, the outcome of which is experiencing a curse; and others do acknowledge God but have not dealt with their problem. This self-negligence of not dealing with their problem causes them to experience the effect of the curse as well. They are not cursed, but because of their self-negligence, they experience the curse, which adds to the hard life they are living. Prisons are also packed with people who have never addressed their wound. Of course, some of the people who are incarcerated in no way have had the opportunity to deal with their issue because of the environment they lived and/or grew up in. They are sick and don't even know it. America has the largest prison population in the world.

Another self-destructive act or infection is the uncontrollable desire to self-medicate or to gratify the pain of an emotional wound with something that seems to give peace and contentment but soon develops into a bad habit. Most of these habits start out pleasurable but the end result is an unmanageable, out-of-control lifestyle.

This unmanageable, out-of-control lifestyle is termed an addiction!

---

3   American Foundation for Suicide Provention http://www.outofthedarkness.org/index.
     cfm?fuseaction=home.viewPage&page_id=A960DCEC-F502-4680-713BDF6AC1E7CE9F

CHAPTER SIX

ADDICTION

Merriam Webster's dictionary defines an addict as:

> Someone with a compulsive need for and use of a habit-forming substance (as heroin, nicotine, or alcohol) characterized by tolerance and by well-defined physiological symptoms upon withdrawal; broadly: persistent compulsive use of a substance known by the user to be harmful.

In other words, an addiction is when a person has established an uncontrollable habit. It's not always restricted to drug use but can be used to describe an unhealthy dominant routine. Human beings are creatures of habit. That's just part of our nature. Any person will cultivate a habit or several habits within his or her lifetime, whether good or bad. Therefore, if someone doesn't discipline him or herself to develop good habits, unhealthy habits will naturally spring up. And when the unhealthy habit becomes uncontrollable, it has became an addiction.

The idolatry I just spoke about in a previous chapter is the twin brother to addiction. Idolatry and addiction are twin brothers! What am I saying? Anything a person consistently gives his or her primary affection to that's not God has become an idol to him or her. When this unhealthy routine of addiction has gotten to the point of dominating your desire, thought life, and emotions, when it is coercing you into directions that you don't want to go, such as a destructive or immoral lifestyle, it has became a god to you. These harmful habits are often used as a tool by demonic spirits to impel the person to wicked actions (Eph. 6:12). In a sense, it is the same principle as worshiping an idol during ancient biblical times. That's how addiction and idolatry are twin brothers. It's the same principle, just a different object; the object in this day and time is often a substance. Of course, there are several other objects of addiction. Some are gambling, sex, pornography, money, etc. The obvious ones, though, are illicit sex, drugs, alcohol, and smoking. However, there are a few things that are addictive that do not rob the person of the place in his or her heart that belongs to God. Some of these are coffee, overeating, and smoking tobacco. They are most definitely *bad for your health* when addiction sets in, but they do not hinder a person's reverence to God.

Drugs

As many of you reading this book already know, crack cocaine has been a primary issue in the United States since the late '70s and early '80s. It was during this time that this new drug emerged. Because of its cheap cost and quick and intense high, crack cocaine quickly gained popularity among users, especially in poor urban areas. Within two decades, the crack had exacted a heavy toll, leaving serious physical and emotional side effects not only on its users, but also on entire communities and on the United States as a whole. Crack is associated with more prostitution, violent crimes, and gang-related crimes than any other drug. The low cost of crack helps explain its rampant spread through poor, urban areas. The highest numbers of crack users are African American men between the ages of eighteen and thirty who come from low socioeconomic backgrounds.

There are also some users that are above the age of thirty. These people are now middle aged and even older and were caught in the first stage of an earlier widespread drug epidemic in the late 1960s through the '70s. They switched addictions to crack in the '80s. Some, though, of that generation were first-time users of crack when it began to surface in the '80s, because society was ignorant of its devastating destruction when it first came on the scene. Even though it was illegal then as it is today, the deception was that it was just a social way of life with no known side effects or the possibility of addiction at that point in time.

Most of the people who are now middle aged that have become addicts began their addiction during the '60s and early '70s—the Vietnam War era. The powerful drugs that were prevalent then were heroin, quaaludes, LSD, acid, window payne, opium, and hash. Of course, these where often mixed with alcohol and marijuana. There was a tremendous amount of emotional pain in society during the Vietnam War that came from the impact of racism, the political fight in the civil rights movement, and the large volume of American soldiers (especially African Americans) who were getting killed in that war. *That generation got hit hard and I mean **hard!*** But the majority of users from any generation don't live to be middle aged if they don't stop their addiction. There are three things that will happen if anyone addicted to drugs continue using them.

1. They either wind up doing a life sentence in prison or on an installment plan, installment meaning in and out of jail and prison for the rest of their lives if they don't get a life sentence from the start.
2. They are disabled from the abuse of the drug or having been seriously injured from an attempt of violence in order to support their addiction.
3. They have died a premature death from an overdose or someone has murdered them in their hustling effort to support the drug habit.

From the time that you awoke this morning and ate some breakfast to start your day up until this point or moment you're reading this book, there have been tons of cocaine moved into and across several states of America. Because of the American climate, coca plants (which is the substance "cocaine" is processed from) will not grow in this country. America is the number one world power on this planet at this particular time in history. It would seem that our law enforcement agencies, the FBI, and the armed forces could stop this drug from crossing the oceans to enter our nation. Customs, the coast guard, the navy, the marine corps, and the CIA all have the ability to monitor all business that is imported and exported into and out of America across the seas. *Now I'm not saying by any means that our government and armed forces are corrupt, because they are not.* But I am implying that evidently there has to be certain people somewhere with big feet. These people have a distorted focus on life (a victim of the curse) that are in high places (authoritative positions) for the extreme quantity—for the sum total—of this drug to enter America.

But by some way, the cocaine travels across the oceans into our society from other parts of the world. Whatever channels are used in this illegal smuggling has avenues that put the majority of this drug into low-income districts throughout our nation, where people are on welfare and food stamps—the poor of this country. Any businessman knows that the little money poor people have has more volatile spending power because the wealth of the richer person is tied up in investments. This paints a picture of intentionally destroying lives, an attempt to control a certain amount of the poor citizens in society and taking control of or redirecting a certain species' destiny. In other words, a type of slavery and selling of human souls still exists, all for the deceptive illusion of money, prestige, and power, which is another element of the curse clearly perceived through this real-life issue. Any of the people who are in authoritative positions in this country who may be involved in drug smuggling are not only ignorant of their place in the curse but are also dominated by demonism (Matt. 4:8–9).

Consider these alarming statistics:

- 10 percent of publicly funded drug abuse center admissions in 2006 were for crack cocaine.

- Approximately 33.7 million Americans ages twelve and older have tried cocaine at least once in their lifetimes (ONDCP).

- One out of four Americans between the age of twenty-six and thirty-four have used cocaine in their lifetime.

- Cocaine is the second most commonly used illicit drug (following marijuana) in the United States. More than 34 million Americans (14.7 percent) age twelve or older have used cocaine at least once in their lifetime (National Survey on Drug Use & Health).

- Over fifteen thousand deaths annually are associated with stimulants in the United States (APA).

- In 1988, about 300,000 infants were born addicted to cocaine.

- During 2004, cocaine was the primary drug involved in federal drug arrests. There were 12,166 federal drug arrests for cocaine in 2004 (ONDCP).

- Cocaine hydrochloride is very stable. It binds closely to the ink in paper currency. FBI chemists have discovered that traces of cocaine can be found on almost every dollar bill in circulation (Drug Enforcement Administration, US Dept. of Justice).

The biblical definition of the term "flesh or corrupt nature" is basically when a person attempts to fill a God-given emotional or physical appetite the way they want to instead of the way God (who is the author of life) has established it to be experienced. The book of Galatians describes the fruits of the flesh in detail.

> Now, the effects of the corrupt nature are obvious: illicit sex, perversion, promiscuity, idolatry, [drug use], hatred, rivalry, jealousy, angry outbursts, selfish ambition, conflict, factions, envy, drunkenness, wild partying, and similar things … (Gal. 5:19–21 God's Word emphasis mine).

The word "drug use" in this verse comes from the Greek word "witchcraft." The New Testament original language is Greek. The root word for witchcraft and sorcery in the Greek is the word *"pharmakia"* which is where we get our English word "pharmacy."

Pharmacies are known for dispensing medication—drugs! Of course, medical doctors and pharmacists are licensed professionals and do their work legally, logically, and for its designed purpose. However, a person who does this illegally is a different story, whether in a business setting (a licensed professional) or illegally on the streets. The US Drug Enforcement Administration (DEA) states:

- Nearly 7 million Americans are abusing prescription drugs—more than the number who are abusing cocaine, heroin, hallucinogens, Ecstasy, and inhalants, combined. That 7 million was just 3.8 million in 2000, an 80 percent increase in just six years.

- Prescription pain relievers are new drug users' drug of choice, rather than marijuana or cocaine.

- Opioid painkillers now cause more drug overdose deaths than cocaine and heroin combined.

- Nearly one in ten high school seniors admits to abusing powerful prescription painkillers. A shocking 40 percent of teens and an almost equal number of their parents think abusing prescription painkillers is safer than abusing "street" drugs.

- Misuse of painkillers represents three-fourths of the overall problem of prescription drug abuse; hydrocodone is the most commonly diverted and abused controlled pharmaceutical in the United States.

- Twenty-five percent of drug-related emergency department visits are associated with abuse of prescription drugs.

- Methods of acquiring prescription drugs for abuse include "doctor-shopping," traditional drug-dealing, theft from pharmacies or homes, illicitly acquiring prescription drugs via the Internet, and from friends or relatives.

Witchcraft as abusive drug use in Galatians 5:20 (KJV) is known for its ritual of mixing potions. *Webster's Dictionary* defines the word potion as "a mixture of liquids (as liquor, chemicals, or medicine)." Any combination of illegal drugs that a person uses or put into his or her body is submitting to the coercion of demonic influences that are behind the deception of social pleasure. *Out of ignorance, these people are opening themselves up to a deeper curse.*

The reason for this is because wicked people who are involved in the art of black magic and other occult practices have conjured up demons, chanted additional curses, and orchestrated demonic assignments to affect this supposedly social activity of drug use. This includes the drug of choice itself having a demonic personality attached to it because it's already a sanction of witchcraft when not used for its intended purpose. In most cases, demonic spirits are never alone. Wherever the action of one is perceived, there is a legion of thousands working in collaboration with the one who has been sighted (Mark 5:1–9 KJV). Legion is an ancient Roman military term that means between three to six thousand troops.

Crack cocaine has attached to it some of Satan's most powerful deceptive demons. Of course, all drug addiction has its roots in the curse, demonism, demonic oppression, or demonic possession. The demons just have different names, personalities, and various levels of immorality depending on the ingredient of the substance, whether methamphetamines, heroin, acid, ecstasy, etc. Whatever way the person acts when intoxicated shows the personality of the demon that's driving him or her. The Bible says that you shall know a tree by the fruit that it bears, meaning that you can tell what's in the heart of a person by the way he or she acts.

Once again, this is not just cocaine; it could be heroin, methamphetamine, alcohol, prescription drugs, or whatever drug a person uses that dominates him or her. The popular drug Ecstasy is a branch of methamphetamine and is just as debilitating as meth. All drugs used during the process of improper abuse and up to the point of addiction, and as long as the person is addicted, are governed by demonic spirits.

Alcohol

The word "alcohol" is derived from the Arabic word *al kuhul*, meaning "essence." "Essence" is a synonym for the word "*spirit*." Alcohol is the favorite mood-altering drug in the United States and in almost every human society. One of the reasons for the significant use of alcohol and its health impact is its feature of being (along with nicotine) a legally available drug of abuse and dependence.

Our knowledge of alcohol rests on a heritage of myth and speculation. Many health benefits have been attributed to alcohol by ancient healers who saw ethanol as the elixir of life, but almost none of its positive benefits have stood the test of time. Alcoholic beverages have been revered, more than any other substance, as mystical and medicinal agents. In recent years, however, we have stripped away much of the mystery surrounding alcohol and now recognize it as a drug with distinct pharmacological effects.

Pharmacology is the study of the changes produced in living animals by chemical substances, especially the actions of drugs. How chemicals affect an animal help scientists determine how it will affect people. However, one of the reasons beverages containing alcohol continue to be consumed socially by the public is the tradition and history that surround its many combinations with other flavors and its many sources of fermentation and distillation. The different brands and flavor of beer, liquor, wine, and even moonshine can be coupled with many things and mixed to a person's taste.

The numerous flavors and brews of alcohol to choose from will add to the easy deception of dominance when being constantly consumed over a period of time. Of course, the alcohol consumption by a person who continually drinks is only a covering of the real issue, the foundation of which is the unhealed emotional wound that has not been faced and dealt with by the consumer.

Listen to how deceptive the role of flavors can be and how they can affect a person in addition to the "*spirit*" of alcohol leading him or her to addiction;

> Don't let the sparkle and the smooth taste of strong wine (alcohol) deceive you. For in the end it bites like a poisonous serpent; it stings like an adder. You will see [hallucinations] and have [delirium tremens], and you will say foolish, silly things that would embarrass you no end when sober. You will stagger like a sailor tossed at sea,

clinging to a swaying mast. And afterwards you will say, "I didn't even know it when they beat me up … *Let's go and have another drink!*" (Prov. 23:31–35 TLB emphasis mine).

I know that this may be hard for some people to grasp as a reality in today's society, but when you consider the uncontrollable, powerless lives of those who are addicted to alcohol, you have to accept the fact that there is something more powerful than they are that has gained control over them.

The above verse tells us not to allow the sparkle and smooth taste of alcohol deceive us, because when you get hooked on it, it will bite you like a snake. In Scripture, the serpent (snake) is used as a symbol for Satan. This celestial being does not have the ability to be omnipresent, so the term serpent can also refer to the many demons that are under his power. In other words, there are way too many alcoholics for the devil to deal with all of them by himself because he can only be in one place at one time. So he has to and does have some help. I believe spiritually that's why alcohol is also call "spirits," because there are many demons that are associated with this substance.

From the ancient historical perspective, the serpent is a creature that was considered to symbolize magic powers, fertility, and powers of darkness. The serpent was the favored symbol of deity of ancient people and is mentioned in the Bible many times. More than a few of those references pertain to the occult.

Secular psychologists and a lot of professionals in the medical field have diagnosed hallucinations as a mental illness, but in all actuality, the truth is that at a certain stage of addiction to alcohol or drugs, a person starts to have a strong perception of the spiritual world. *Drugs and alcohol facilitate spirit communication!*

In many cases, what has been termed as "hallucination" is the alcoholic seeing and communicating with demons and their influence. The delirium tremens (known as DTs) is a psychosis of chronic alcoholism, usually due to alcohol withdrawal, which can be fatal. Hallucinations, insomnia, and disorientation are part of the withdrawal symptoms when the person is being freed from this particular curse that's also driven by demonic oppression or possession. These "spirits" are being forced to leave the body because of detoxing. Once again, these symptoms include sweating, tremors, terrifying hallucinations, insomnia, restlessness, disorientation, and anxiety. The medical field call delirium tremens a psychosis because alcoholism can leave a severe mental disorder, sometimes with physical damage to the brain, marked by a deranged personality and a distorted view of reality. This is only one of many dangers of prolonged activity with alcohol and the "spirits" that are intimate with it. The other danger of alcoholism is the premature deterioration of the body and its body parts. Some of these are liver, kidney, intestinal, and stomach diseases that can be fatal.

Smoking

Tobacco eventually leads to death or disability for half of all regular users. Nevertheless, about 47 million adults in the United States smoke cigarettes. Four out of five adults who smoked began by age eighteen. The majority of people who do not begin smoking at a young age will most likely never start to smoke.

Smoking was probably first practiced by the indigenous peoples of the Western Hemisphere. Originally used in religious rituals and in some instances for medicinal purposes, smoking and the use of tobacco became a widespread practice by the late 1500s (www.encyclopedia.com smoking).

Early modern tobacco style varied by geography, class, and local custom; some users preferred pipes, others chewing tobacco, and others snuff. Today tobacco is another drug of addiction, whether smoking or chewing. This product is not usually driven by demonic forces, and neither is it a curse, even though it was used primitively in religious rituals by the Indians.

Research has discovered that tobacco use is something that a person has started to do to unknowingly gratify the pain of an emotional wound. It is a learned habit. Because of addictive organic chemicals that cause a relaxing effect on the mind and nervous system, it is easily developed into a habit, and that habit is bad for your health. Yes! It is a bad habit that in a lot of cases is extremely difficult to break. But there is hope for those who are having a difficult time breaking the habit, because it can be overcome.

Tobacco contains a chemical known as nicotine (NIK-o-teen). Smokers can become addicted to this substance, which means they can become dependent on it physically and suffer unpleasant symptoms when it is taken away. For some people, the addiction to nicotine is as strong as that to heroin or cocaine. In fact, when nicotine is inhaled in cigarette smoke, it reaches the brain even faster than drugs that enter the body through a vein.

So basically, nicotine, a naturally occurring constituent of tobacco, is the active ingredient in tobacco smoke. The amount of nicotine in tobacco leaves ranges from approximately 2 percent to 7 percent. In concentrated form, it is used as an insecticide, and we all know that an insecticide is a chemical agent used to destroy insect pests. Nicotine, which mimics the effects of acetylcholine, acts primarily on the autonomic nervous system. This is what gives its users a false sense of peace and calmness. However, there is danger. In a dose of less than 50 mg, it can cause respiratory failure and general paralysis. Smaller toxic doses can cause heart palpitations, lowered blood pressure, nausea, and dizziness. *A person who smokes inhales approximately 3 mg from one cigarette. This amount increases the heart rate, constricts the blood vessels, and acts on the central nervous system, imparting a feeling of alertness and well-being.*

In the United States, there are more people who die from nicotine in one year than all of the deaths caused by illegal drugs put together. Tobacco use is the primary cause of preventable death, leading to more than 400,000 deaths each year. It kills more people than AIDS, alcohol, drug abuse, car crashes, murders, suicides, and fires combined (www. encyclopedia.com/).

Nicotine is a poisonous, pale yellow, oily liquid alkaloid with a pungent odor and an acrid taste. It turns brown on exposure to air. Alkaloid is an addictive organic chemical that also is found in morphine, cocaine, quinine, caffeine, strychnine, serotonin, and LSD.

Habitual tobacco use can cause chronic bronchitis, emphysema, heart disease, stroke, and several cancers.

Cigarette smoke contains more than four thousand different chemicals, and more than forty of these have been shown to cause cancer in humans and animals. Smokers are more likely to get several kinds of cancer, including that of the mouth, larynx, esophagus, bladder, cervix, pancreas, and kidney.

Smoking and other addictions are the result of self-medicating the wound of emotional pain. Some of these pains have been caused by the various traumas in life. Most of the addictions and bad habits of people are cultivated not knowing the source. Nearly everyone who is addicted started out with the desire to be physically or emotionally gratified and was not aware that it was the subtle effect of their emotional pain causing it. As noted earlier in chapter five, a lot of these wounds generally begin and are experienced in childhood.

CHAPTER SEVEN

BAD HABITS

All bad habits are not a result of the curse, neither are they all interrelated with a curse. However, a bad habit can be a tool used against a person by unclean spirits if the habit is not broken and managed. The difference between an addiction and a bad habit is that an addiction is demonically driven. A person who is addicted may be either possessed or oppressed by evil spirits. But a bad habit is self-induced and self-driven. Nevertheless, there is a thin line between a bad habit and an addiction. In other words, a bad habit can cross over into an addiction.

Bad habits are also an imperfect bandage for an emotional wound. Not only are they an imperfect cover up for a wound, but they also can come from not being disciplined into practicing good behavior. Remember, human beings are creatures of habit, and if a person does not practice good habits, bad ones will naturally set in.

A bad habit can weigh you down instead of causing you to fly, fly in the sense of operating at the maximum potential of your purpose for being alive. There can be crippling, hidden habits that can prevent you from going to the height, from attaining the altitude of success in which you can soar. Great men have great habits. They have daily practices that set them apart from the masses. A person's habits are a major part of the equation of shaping a successful future, and on the other hand, they play a vital part in a person living a defeated life. There are habits that will sink you like the *Titanic*.

A working definition for a habit is; "a pattern of behavior that is acquired by frequent repetition." This kind of conduct will reveal the prevailing character of a person, prevailing in the sense of showing a person where his or her life is headed because of his or her consistent negative actions. It eventually becomes the makeup of that person's character. We all come into this world with natural inclinations to sin. We've already learned that we've inherited this moral dysfunction from Adam and Eve. The problem is that many of us have allowed these inclinations to become bad habits because we attempt to feed the desire to be loved and accepted with a continued temporary gratification instead of an active relationship with a God who is love. The next thing you know, a bad habit has been formed.

A habit can be hell's greatest weapon in destroying your life. One of the things God's enemy wants us to do is to develop destructive habits. By doing so, he won't have to take us out; we will do it ourselves. Not only can a bad habit give birth to chronic diseases, which are one way of taking our own selves out, but morally bad habits have caused people to murder and assault one another. For example, America is facing an epidemic of homicide among young black males. According to a recent 2010 study conducted by Professor James Alan Fox of Northeastern University, one of the nation's leading criminal justice researchers, from 2002 to 2007, the number of black male juvenile homicide victims rose by 31 percent. The number of young black homicide victims killed by guns rose at an even sharper rate: 54 percent

It is God's desire for a person to confront his or her own personal habits, whether they are noticeable or hidden. There are some things that you realize are serving as a weight in your life that's holding you down and prohibiting you from soaring to the height that God desires for you. This bad habit could be a number of things, but you of all people know better than anyone else the thing you are wrestling with. Life works when you live it according to God's rules, not when you go out of bounds and choose to do things your way. Life becomes challenging when you decide to do it your way, continue in that pattern, and develop a destructive habit. Of course, most people won't agree with it being destructive because it feels good to do it, to practice it, and to apply it. But in the end, it is bitter and will cut into your heart like a sharp razor damaging your life. Depending on the type of habit it is, most people would not even want to be around you. The end can be a life of solitude in old age.

When negative impulses are not controlled, they eventually grow into habits, and when these inclinations grow, some of them can be life threatening and as we said earlier, can become addictions. It starts with an impulse, moves to a habit, and then becomes an addiction driven by a demon holding you captive by a curse.

A German shepherd can be trained to rip your hand apart if you stick it into a fence. It can be trained to be a ferocious counterpart to evil intent. Yet that same highly intelligent animal can be taught to be a helpful companion to an eighty-two-year-old blind woman by helping her to cross the street: same animal, same dog, same breed. One will rip off your hand or whole arm; the other will safely take a blind lady across the street. Same animal! So what's the difference? I'll tell you the difference! Trained behavior!

There is one person who is in medical school, and another is on crack cocaine. Two kids can grow up in the same house yet go in totally different directions. What's the difference? One is trained behavior, and the other is learned behavior. In the same way, bad habits are learned behaviors that turn into powerful forces in a person's life. Every habit is either a virtue (a developed good habit) or a vice (an undisciplined, self-learned behavior). Lifestyles will enhance you or enslave you; they can be a beauty or become a beast.

Salvation is one thing, but deliverance is something else. And some of God's people need to adhere to this. There are a lot of people who are saved but are bound. In other words, you can be saved but not delivered from bad habits. Here are some questions that are a checklist to determine if you are already trapped in or maybe developing the wrong type of habits that can become a life-threatening addiction.

1. Are your thoughts consumed with it? Are you always thinking about it?
2. Is your time scheduled around it? Do you look for an opportunity to squeeze it in?
3. Could your health be harmed by it? Is this desire adding to your life, or is it assisting dehumanization?
4. Does it increase your guilt? In other words, do you feel a stronger shame after you've completed the act?
5. Are your finances affected by it? How much does your routine cost?
6. Are you defensive when you're asked about it? Are you in denial?
7. Are your relationships hurt by it? Do you honor the action more than the people you love?

That's how habits are; they are unhealthy behavior patterns that have become so consistent through repetition that they often become the prevailing character of a person. The character from the fruit of a bad habit will govern your whole life. It will eventually dictate the actions in every area of your life: mentally, emotionally, financially, and spiritually. There are so many people that have habits that have their relationships all messed up. They are missing time with their children; kids are growing old without even intimately knowing their parents. And sometimes there's a mother or a father who's caught up in a selfish, time-consuming, self-gratifying condition that affects the trust of children.

And this can't be said enough, because children are tomorrow's future leaders and participants of this world. However, there are scores of bad habits that are a result of a person's childhood experiences. It is an amazing fact that family members, friends, and various lifestyles in society can have a powerful negative impact on children. But as a child grows older, he or she can begin to decide the habits they want to cultivate, if they are in a productive environment that has positive leadership that understands trained and learned behavior. If they're not in this type of environment, it makes it more difficult for them to correctly grow mentally and emotionally.

There are many, many young people who have been robbed of moral parents as well as role models because of bad habits. Consequently, they are growing up majoring on minors, focusing on objects that don't really matter. They're trying to get gold and platinum and rims, and none of that stuff can take you to success in life.

However, when you are no longer a child, you do not have to be controlled or influenced by the attitude and actions of other people. Your personal attitude properly nourished by anointed leadership, discipline, and right choices is a vital ingredient in the equation of success. It will increase the altitude of your life's purpose. You can choose to plant, and you can choose to cultivate and harvest good habits that are desirable and pleasing to God. Whatever you do, every day is what you will have the potential to develop in. If you look back over your life, you will see that what you have become today is what you have been doing each day in the past. You are right now the final product of your daily actions.

If you lie every day, you will become a liar by natural instinct. It will become second nature to you; you will be a developed liar. I'm sure you know some. If you steal every day, you will become a developed thief. If you watch pornography every day, you will form a perverted sexual addiction.

And if you're married, you will subconsciously expect your wife or husband to perform like the people you have been watching in the pornography, and certain sexual acts may not be in your spouse's character. Therefore, you are damaging your most important relationship. If you gamble every day, you will become a developed gambler. Whatever you do every day, that's what you have the potential to develop in. It will form in your personality, and that's what you will eventually become!

A good, healthy thing for you to do right now is ask yourself the question, "What am I really doing every day?"

You need to ask this question and be brutally honest with yourself because whatever you're doing each day is what you have the potential to become. You are self-developing in that area or areas. Yes! I say areas because there are some people who are gifted in multitasking, and you surely want to manage your life instead of having multiple uncontrollable bad habits dominating you. This is especially true if the habits are developed to the point of addiction and being demonically driven by multiple demons.

So basically, a person should establish his or her habits, and the result would be that their habits will compose their life. In other words, you make your habits, and your habits will make your life. There are a lot of individuals who are wonderful people on the surface, but within themselves are hidden habits. And these un-dealt-with habits are a type of fuel or tool the enemy (Satan) uses to flaw their own character. They have done it to themselves. Most people you first meet are not really the person you're talking to because of hidden bad habits. Remember, habits (good or bad) are what define a person's current character.

Again, there are a lot of individuals who are wonderful people on the surface, but within themselves are hidden habits. Oftentimes it's not easy to see or recognize this dysfunction until you get to know the person. Have you ever wondered why some people are not as nice as they were when you first met them? That's because at first, you didn't meet the real them, you met their representative, so to speak. You communicated with the "mask" (pre-formed personality) that people wear to cover up the hidden habit they're harboring. That's who people are pretending to be in public; that's who they want you to know. After spending time with them, you will discover that there is somebody else living in that body. It's not the person you were led to believe it to be. Every person is the sum total of their habits or hungers. The Bible says:

> For they that are after the flesh do mind the things of the flesh; but they that are after the Spirit the things of the Spirit.
>
> For to be carnally minded *is* death; but to be spiritually minded *is* life and peace (Rom. 8:5–6 KJV).

We will look at how a person's thinking controls his or her actions later on in this book, but for now, in this verse, can you see how a person's thinking shows up in how he or she acts? This passage of Scripture explains how a person who's after the "flesh" (that is seeking selfish gratification) keeps these desires in his or her mind. Selfish gratification is the person's primary focus. What people think is what they will do, and we've already learned that what someone does every day develops that action to be in his or her character. It becomes the person, part of who he or she is! If fleshly, self-gratifying desires are all you're thinking about, then that's how you're going to live.

But the last part of verse 5 says that they who are after the Spirit, seeking the things of God, do and keep the things of God in mind. The next verse implies that a person who is carnally minded (focused on selfish gratification that's become a bad habit) can die a premature death. But those who are spiritually minded have life and peace. Life and peace are the things that everybody on earth is looking for.

Now the revelation in the next verse of chapter eight tells us that people who are focused on keeping these bad, self-gratifying habits make themselves enemies of God.

> Focusing on the self is the opposite of focusing on God. Anyone completely absorbed in self ignores God, ends up thinking more about self than God. That person ignores who God is and what he is doing (Rom. 8:7 TM).

The same verse in the King James Version reads:

> Because the carnal (self gratifying) mind *is* enmity against God: for it is not subject to the law of God, neither indeed can be (Rom. 8:7 KJV emphasis mine).

This does not include the people whose hearts desire to be freed from the crippling bondage of a bad habit, but those who enjoy it and want to continue holding onto it. Someone who is wrestling, struggling, and fighting for his or her life to be corrected is a different story. This is not the case with people who are ready to delve into their mess as soon and frequently as they can. God knows your heart. I'm sure you know that it's impossible to fool God. Heart issues are God issues. He knows what's on your mind before you do!

> O LORD, thou hast searched me, and known *me*. Thou knowest my downsitting and mine uprising, *thou understandest my thought afar off.* Thou compassest my path and my lying down, and art *acquainted with all my ways. For there is not a word in my tongue, but, lo, O LORD, thou knowest it altogether.* Thou hast beset me behind and before, and laid thine hand upon me. *Such* knowledge *is* too wonderful for me; it is high, I cannot *attain* unto it (Ps. 139:1–6 KJV emphasis mine).

God knows exactly where you are at and what you are struggling with. There is no miracle cure for the flesh like there is for physical healing and other supernatural acts. This spiritual war is a lifelong battle. The apostle Paul says:

> I find, then, the law, that when I desire to do what is right, with me the evil is present (Rom. 7:21 YLT).

However, the victory is already won, and we have the overcoming provisions to conquer bad habits through Jesus Christ. That's why it is so crucial to develop good habits, because there is no miracle cure for these fleshly inclinations that every person has, but we can rule over them by the power of God's Holy Spirit and practice. Remember, what a person does is what he or she will become. There are so many people who have never been taught the importance of surveying or taking an inventory on what they are hungering for that have now become bad habits in their life.

All of these bad character-forming habits come from people who unknowingly attempt to heal the hurt and the emotional pain that's in their heart. Until you *"move past your pain,"* it is practically impossible to maintain continual freedom from a bad habit or an addiction, because the fuel of the fire of an unmanageable life is still in your tank ready to be ignited. And that fuel that is waiting to be ignited is a wounded heart.

The Spirit of the Lord *is* upon me, because he hath anointed me to preach the gospel to the poor; he hath sent me to heal the brokenhearted, to preach deliverance to the captives, and recovering of sight to the blind, to set at liberty them that are bruised, To preach the acceptable year of the Lord. Luke 4:18-19 (KJV)

CHAPTER EIGHT

MOVING PAST YOUR PAIN

Now that we understand that everyone at some point in their life will experience various traumas of emotional pain, the question to ask yourself is, "Have I personally addressed any past hurts that I may be still harboring?" If not, then your wound could possibly be festering over into your relationships as well as being the source to any addiction or bad habit you are exhibiting. Anger, lashing out, addiction, and bad habits are tools the enemy uses to keep you in bondage and the prey of certain curses. In addition to this, the source as well as the acting out of curses can unknowingly be passed on through your family from one generation to the next.

Remember, wounds could have been inflicted by some type of neglect from your parents, or it could have been inflicted by some kind of mental, physical, or verbal abuse. Words are one of the most powerful forces on earth. The Bible says that death and life are in the power of the tongue (Prov. 18:21). Someone could have inflicted continual verbal abuse upon you while growing up. It could have been through peer pressure at school. There also may be some emotional scars as a result of being victimized by sexual abuse. Then there are people who are just generally mean and do stuff to people just for the spite of it, without realizing the crippling effect it can have on the victim. Usually these are people who have never faced their wounds. Remember, "Hurt people, hurt people." Your pain could have come from a nasty broken relationship or from some unfilled promises that were made to you that did not happen or from some major moral failures. Some of you may even desire to break away from cult or occult practices or may be the victim of flat-out spiritual curses that may have been directed on you by wicked people who are living and functioning in satanic worship, witchcraft, black magic, or some form of demonic activity.

Whatever the case, all of these inflictions can cut into your soul like a sharp knife and cause terrible, devastating emotional pain that will linger for a lifetime if not faced and dealt with. Many people who will not deal with their issues are like debris that gets caught up in the whirlwind of a tornado. Just as the whirlwind of a terrible storm may sling the debris from houses, trees, and other material anywhere and in any direction, so can the whirlwind of an unhealed wound cause you to be tossed around and land in destructive places in life—places you don't want to really go, be, or live.

There are ten major principles that are vital to your deliverance and emotional healing that I want to go over with you. Conversely, the one mother wound of all wounds—that is, the underlying wound—of every human when he or she is born into this world is separation from God. Bear in mind that because of the disobedience to God by Adam and Eve, the whole human race is separated from God, even at birth. This is a major dysfunction that has been inherited by all of us because we are the descendants of the first human beings.

> And the LORD God commanded the man, saying, Of every tree of the garden thou mayest freely eat: But of the tree of the knowledge of good and evil, thou shalt not eat of it: *for in the day that thou eatest thereof thou shalt surely die* (Gen. 2:16–17 KJV).

This historical record of the human race goes on to inform us that after God created and instructed the man, He then prepared and presented to the man a wife (Gen. 2:18, 21–25). She eventually carried on a conversation with God's enemy, who coerced her into eating from the tree that God had instructed the man not to eat from (Gen. 3:1–6). As a result, judgment and curses were sanctioned (Gen. 3:14–19). Separation from God was also the consequence of disobedience because of His holiness.

> And the LORD God said, Behold, the man is become as one of us, to know good and evil: and now, lest he put forth his hand, and take also of the tree of life, and eat, and live forever: Therefore the LORD God sent him forth from the garden of Eden, to till the ground from whence he was taken. *So he drove out the man; and he placed at the east of the garden of Eden Cherubims, and a flaming sword which turned every way, to keep the way of the tree of life* (Gen. 3:22–24, emphasis KJV).

This expulsion from the Garden of Eden included being evicted from the presence of the tree of life. The tree of life was then, and still is, protected by cherubim, which are guardian angels for God.

When God said that man has become as one of us to know good and evil, He knew that the man would carry out any evil he wanted too as a result of selfishness or anger. We learned this when Cain murdered his brother Abel (Gen, 1:4–8). God is the only entity who knows evil but does the right thing all of the time. It is because of God's holiness that He separated the man from His presence. Evil cannot dwell with the holiness of God or He wouldn't be holy. Remember, the word "holy" means free from moral evil and the word "moral" means right and wrong behavior sanctioned by conscious and ethical judgment. Ethical judgment as it pertains to God again implies that God knows evil, and as I have already stated, He always chooses to do the right thing. The human race can't do what is right on a consistent basis because of selfishness and the familiarity with the deceitfulness of evil. The knowledge of evil in the mind and heart of Adam and Eve resulted in their separation from God, which has affected as well as infected every human being.

When the mental comprehension of the man and his wife had changed because of the evil in their heart, they realized that they were naked and attempted to hide from God because they were ashamed. God then clothed them both out of animal skin.

> Unto Adam also and to his wife did the LORD God make coats of skins, and clothed them (Gen. 3:21 KJV).

The act of this clothing symbolizes (at the early stage of God's plan to reconcile humanity back to Him) the covering of "holiness" we receive through Jesus Christ that makes us holy and acceptable in the sight and presence of God.

> And you that were sometime alienated (separated) and enemies in *your* mind by wicked works (the knowledge of evil inherited from the first humans), yet now hath he reconciled In the body of his flesh through death (Jesus Christ), *to present you holy and unblameable and unreproveable in his sight* (Col. 1:21–22, KJV emphasis mine).

It is through the acceptance of the life, death, burial, and resurrection of Jesus Christ that a person is re-united to God. So until a person receives

Jesus as his or her personal Lord and Savior, he or she is born into this world separated from God.

Again, this is the mother wound of all wounds that has caused devastating turmoil throughout the world in the lives of people who choose not to deal with it. Actually, since the beginning of time, neglecting God has resulted in dangerous consequences for individuals, families, and nations.

So here are ten principles that are extremely vital for your deliverance and emotional healing:

1. *First of all, you have to believe that Jesus really desires to heal and deliver you.*

How you deal with your pain has a lot to do with knowing what Jesus came to do with it, because there is an anointing Jesus proclaims that deals with pain at every level of its impact. In Luke 4, Jesus testifies of His mission and purpose.

Jesus announces:

> The Spirit of the Lord *is* upon me, because he hath anointed me to preach the gospel to the [poor]; he hath sent me to heal the [brokenhearted], to preach *deliverance to the captives,* and *recovering of sight to the blind,* to set at [liberty] them that are [bruised], To preach the acceptable year of the Lord (Luke 4:18–19 KJV, emphasis mine).

Now let's look at the progression of pain that He expresses deliverance from as I translate this passage for you. Jesus was saying that there was an anointing upon His life to preach good news to people in a bad situation. *The word "gospel" means good news.*

When He spoke of *poverty,* He was not speaking of a people who had a lack of finance but of those who were *spiritually and emotionally bankrupt. You must know and remember that poverty is never a condition but always a mindset.* King David, for example, was not financially poor; he was the king. But he was acknowledging that he had a state of mind that was inconsistent with what God wanted him to have because he was wounded.

> For I *am* poor and needy, and my heart is [wounded] within me (Ps. 109:22 KJV, emphasis mine).

So basically, if my head isn't right, then my heart won't be. This type of *"poverty"* can result in low or no finances, but more likely in low self-esteem and depression (Ps. 109: 21–25).

In addition to the mother wound (being born into the world separated from God) coupled with the additional wounds a person may come into in life, many of us experience a *broken heart*. Healing the *brokenhearted* is part of Jesus's mission too. Having a broken heart usually relates to the grief of having a broken relationship.

He then tells us that those who are in some type of *captivity* are also included in His deliverance. He was implying that if a person's *head* is not where it should be, it results in the *poverty* of *low self-esteem, depression, and a broken heart*; a broken heart because their relationships are not healthy. This condition makes them vulnerable, and they are taken captive by different vices. We've already learned that these vices include bad habits, addiction, and curses. A few more vices to note are prison time and cultic and occult practices. Remember this word of wisdom: *"Attitude determines altitude."* The attitudes you entertain today indicate what you are in the *process* of becoming tomorrow … and in old age.

When a person's mindset is not right, he or she has a distorted perception of spiritual reality, so Jesus also came to give us a clear understanding of life, which is the recovering of sight to the blind. This means that a person can't perceive in his or her mind's eye the truth about life. And without a *conversant* (meaning active) relationship with Jesus Christ, this insight is totality impossible.

So when the perception of Jesus's mission, purpose, and provisions are realized and implemented into your life, then He has set at liberty or freed those whose hearts have been *bruised* by blows of their wound. He came to set at liberty those who are bruised (Luke 4:19b). *Once your head is out, once your heart is out, then you've got to come out!*

In the book of Mark, Jesus says:

> They that are whole have no need of the physician, but they that are sick: I came not to call the righteous, but sinners to repentance (Mark 2:17 KJV).

Basically, what Jesus is saying is that He came to deal with your issues. His purpose was not only to re-unite us to God but to help those of us who have problems. You've got to know and be confident that this is what the intention of His ministry is to you and me.

When Jesus walked the face of this earth, He was confronted with the same things we encounter, but He overcame them. In other words, He can empathize and relate to what's wrong with us, what we are dealing with, and what we are going through. Scripture informs us:

> For we have not an high priest (meaning Jesus) which cannot be touched with the feeling of our infirmities; but was in all points tempted like as *we are, yet* without sin. *Let us therefore come boldly unto the throne of grace, that we may obtain mercy, and find grace to help in time of need* (Heb. 4:15–16 KJV, emphasis mine).

By the grace of God, we have a Savior who can identify with our pain. He knows your hurt and what you are going through. When you study and look into the Word, you will discover that Jesus taught us how to go through the trauma that causes emotional pain. Jesus was lied about; He was talked about, laughed at, persecuted, and betrayed. The life of Jesus gives us some powerful lessons on managing our emotions. And it is the anointing of His Holy Spirit in us that gives us the ability to overcome the hurt.

The last part of this verse tells us that we can boldly come into God's presence to get help in time of need. So there is no need to tiptoe to God when you pray. Just come straight to Him knowing that He is waiting on you to bring Him the pain, the problem, and the issue. God has the exact prescription for what you are going through.

2. ***You must come out of denial and openly acknowledge and confess your wound.***

Let me make this statement to you: "It's okay to say this stuff hurts!" Many of us want to be heroes for someone else, like our spouse and children. This is rightfully so, but it is crippling to yourself when at the same time you are hiding your pain. It's not healthy to harbor your pain because you don't want anybody to think that you are weak or a pushover. You have to come out of denial and accept the fact that this stuff, the pain you have in you, hurts. God wants us to trust in Him as well as pour out our heart to Him in confessing our pain.

> Trust in him at all times; *ye* people, pour out your heart before him: God *is* a refuge for us (Ps. 62:8 KJV).

In other words, when you go and pray, stop being in denial and pour your pain out to God. The psalmist said:

> I called upon the LORD in distress: the LORD answered me, *and set me* in a large place. The LORD *is* on my side; I will not fear: what can man do unto me? (Ps. 118:5–6 KJV).

When King David was saying in this Psalm that he called upon the Lord in his distress, he was implying that he called on God in his pain and his problem. A powerful nugget in this verse says, *"The Lord is on my side; I will not fear. What can man do unto me?"*

People will often talk big if they're on a team with a famous celebrity, whether it is sports, a card game, or whatever. I mean, just imagine if Michael Jordan was on your basketball squad in the hood. Most likely, you couldn't shut up bragging about it. But you have the Creator of the universe on your side. That's something to shout about! The apostle Paul in the book of Romans tells us:

> What shall we then say to these things? If God *be* for us, who *can be* against us? He that spared not his own Son, but delivered him up for us all, how shall he not with him also freely give us all things? (Rom. 8:31–32 KJV).

Let me break this passage of Scripture down for you. It is basically telling you, *"If God is for you, no one else has a choice or a chance against you!"*

You don't have to go through life scared of what people may say or try to do against you because God is on your side. You can come out of denial with confidence and be honest with yourself and God about your issue.

3. *You must have the courage to face the pain and the ugliness of the wound.*

This seems like it could be a hard thing for you to do, but you can do it. The Holy Spirit has given you the ability to accomplish this. Plus, if you know that God is on your side, then that should strengthen your motivation too. You just have to choose to make the effort. Therefore, you need to be brutally honest with yourself and decide to deal with your issue with your whole heart. If someone says to you (depending on who's doing the speaking), "How are you doing today?" don't say, "Everything is all right" when it's not. Or someone may say, "Do you want to talk about it?" Don't answer, "No! Let's talk about something else." *Learn to calmly express your feelings and get the pain out of you.*

There are two types of people when it comes to the healing of a wound: implosive and explosive. The explosive people are the ones who will just go on and get it out of their system and get it over with. The implosive people are the ones who will scare you. They are the ones who will just hold the pain in, and hold it in, and hold it in. Then one day something will happen that will trigger the anger that has built up in them, and those are the ones who will snap or go ballistic on you. So it is extremely important that you face your wound and its pain no matter how ugly it is.

4. *You must deal with the root and not just the symptom.*

It is vital to your healing that you get to the core issue of your problem. If people only deal with the symptoms, their predicament will never be resolved but will continue to resurface. The danger for some people, though, is that they can unknowingly be dealing with the symptoms and assuming that they are progressing to restoration. It can easily be a self-deception if you don't get right down to the root of the dilemma.

In every miracle Jesus performed, He went directly to the root. One instance that comes to mind is when He spoke to a fig tree.

> And on the morrow, when they were come from Bethany, he was hungry: And seeing a fig tree afar off having leaves, he came, if haply he might find anything thereon: and when he came to it, he found nothing but leaves; for the time of figs was not *yet*. And Jesus answered and said unto it, No man eat fruit of thee hereafter forever. And his disciples heard *it* ... And in the morning, as they passed by, they saw the fig tree **dried up from the roots**. And Peter calling to remembrance saith unto him, Master, behold, the fig tree which thou [cursedst] is *withered away* (Mark 11:12–14, 20–21 KJV emphasis mine).

The root is how a tree gets its nutrients, nourishment, minerals, and stability from the dirt coupled with the sun to live and stand strong. So it is with you if you don't get to the source of your issue. It will have the potential nourishment to live on inside of you. You will be just like a tree with a limb cut off, meaning that your problem will still be growing and thriving against you, just with some misplaced or shifted areas.

There are many spiritual gifts that operate and/or function through the members of the body of Christ. However, there have been certain burdens that have been cast upon the pastor, deacon, elder, or a member of the congregation that they are not qualified to do. Don't misunderstand me, but what the Church has historically done was put something on a person that he or she was not prepared to do when it comes to getting down to the root of certain issues.

People may want to talk to their pastor or one of their church leaders about an issue they may have, and that's a good and right thing to do. But! All they can share with you is what's in the Bible. In any healing, in any change, the knowledge of the Word of God has to be part of the equation for the healing to acquire its proper effect. However, legally, the church has to stay inside the parameters of the word.

In other words, we have put a stigma on clinical and Christian counseling. We have made people think that they have a lack of faith or that they were crazy for going to therapy, when in fact, without clinical or Christian counseling, a lot of us would not get to the root of our problem.

There are many people who get exhilarated by hearing a powerful word preached, scream "Hallelujah," and fall out, but when they get up and church is over, they still have their problem because they never got counseling or clinical therapy to get rid of their root. *That's why the same people keep joining church every Sunday.*

It's okay to go talk to somebody, to find a good Christian counselor. You're getting the Word at church, but in a several cases, the church leaders are not clinical therapists, which may be needed to get to the root of your dilemma.

5. *You have to forgive and let it go!*

Jesus taught us in the gospels that if we don't forgive our fellow human beings, neither will our father who is in heaven forgive us.

> But if ye forgive not men their trespasses, neither will your
> Father forgive your trespasses (Matt. 6:15 KJV).

Holding resentment and harboring bitterness against people that have offended you, even victimized you, will keep you in the bondage of your pain. I fully understand that this is not easy if you have been victimized. But you must work through the discipline of implementing forgiveness. If not, it will actually add more injury to the infliction of your wound, and it's like throwing gasoline on the fire of any other unhealed wound you may have. Yes! There are some people who are crippled by multiple wounds.

Another danger of unforgiveness to consider is that your life will continue to be stagnant. You may seem like you are progressing because of the physical, everyday action of eating, sleeping, working, and various other activities throughout the day, but the truth of the matter is that your life will be spiritually stuck. You will continue to be in that same emotional condition—just getting older.

> His own iniquities shall take the wicked himself, and he shall be holden (held) with the cords (ropes) of his sins (unforgiveness). He shall die without instruction; and in the greatness of his folly (foolishness) he shall go astray (Prov. 5:22–23 KJV, emphasis mine).

Unforgiveness can cause people to do things with the wrong motive in their heart, which is what iniquity is. It also will cause you to slander others, as well as wishing something bad would happen to them and not realizing that this type of character is wicked no matter how justifiable it may seem to you. These kinds of emotions are spiritual ropes that will tie you up and hold you back from progressing. This passage of Scripture also says that if people don't take heed to the art of forgiving, they will die without having received the instructions of life. They will go to their grave when their time on earth is up having never experienced the true meaning and effect of life, which is how to spread love and be a reflection of their Creator the way God designed life to be lived.

The apostle Paul explains in the book of Colossians how we are to respond to each other, mainly to those who have offended you.

> Put on therefore, as the elect of God, holy and beloved, bowels of mercies, kindness, humbleness of mind, meekness, longsuffering; forbearing one another, and forgiving one another, *if any man have a quarrel against any: even as Christ forgave you, so also do ye.* And above all these things *put on* charity (*love*), which is the bond of perfectness (*maturity*). And let the peace of God rule in your hearts, to the which also ye are called in one body; and be ye thankful (Col. 3:12–15 KJV, emphasis mine).

6. **Live in Love**

Love is the greatest sign of maturity. God has too much for you to continue to hold on to stuff people have done to you. You have to let it go for your own benefit! Then you can go on and progress in your life, you can live and maximize your God-given potential. This doesn't mean that you have to forget what was done to you but to let it go! Keep yourself lifted up in prayer, and discipline yourself to get over it. God has commanded us to love our enemies. Praying and applying this passage of Scripture will increase your prayer life.

> But I say unto you, [Love] your enemies, [bless] them that curse you, do good to them that hate you, and [pray] for them which despitefully use you, and persecute you (Matt. 5:44 KJV).

If you start thinking about everybody who has hurt you, offended you, and talked about you, you ought to be on your face every day asking God to forgive and bless him or her.

God is actually telling us to love it out of them. Hurt people that hurt people have so much hell in them that God's wisdom is telling us to love the hell out of them. Learn to be nice to your haters! Pray for them, and leave the consequences to God.

7. **Find a safe place to take off your mask.**

We all know that a mask is something that is worn to cover the face. In other words, people can hide their true appearance by wearing a mask, which makes it difficult to see the real them. So it is with someone who will not choose to acknowledge their pain and find a safe place to discuss their personal faults. They will be living one way, as though everything is fine, but in their heart living out and practicing the thing that's destroying them. They are living another way and groaning with pain while hiding the effect of a trauma and at the same time falsely pretending to be someone they are not.

James 5:16 tells us:

> Confess *your* faults one to another, and pray one for another, that ye may be healed. The effectual fervent prayer of a righteous man availeth much (James 5:16 KJV).

This is about accountability! Who in your life can you trust and be accountable to? Who in your life can you call and say, "I need some help with this"? You need to have at least two or three people in your life who can objectively look at your situation who you can truly trust. Someone who doesn't have an angle, who doesn't have a negative motive, but someone who can truly hold you accountable for the better as you confess your faults.

Remember that you can't do this just anywhere or talk to just anybody because other people may still be wearing their mask too. Most of all, you may not want to do it with the people you hang out with because they may talk too much. You know, the person who comes up and says, "I know I'm not supposed to tell anybody, don't tell so and so I said this, but ..."

Now, if they are telling you this about someone else, just think about what they will say to somebody about you. Therefore, choose someone you can trust who can be a safe place to take off your mask, confess your faults to, and who will honestly hold you accountable for your well being.

8. *Find comfort and strength in God's Word.*

God's Word is powerful! In the Bible are spoken the same powerful words that were spoken in creation when God created heaven and earth. When He said, "Let there be light," we see the same daylight that was created centuries ago every day today. When He spoke to the sun and commanded it to function, we see the same sun that was created centuries ago still obeying His commands. When God told Adam that in the day you eat from the tree of the knowledge of good and evil you shall surely die, not only did Adam eventually die, but people are still dying every day. He told Adam and Eve to be fruitful and multiply, and they had children, and babies are still being born into this world every day.

What am I saying? The words in the Bible are so powerful because they were spoken by God. They are still in effect and correspond with our reality because we are living inside of everything He said. In other words, what God said then is still so today, and you and I are part of it. Actually, it's common sense.

When a person sincerely looks to the Author of life by seeking Him in His Word with his or her whole heart, He makes known to them His presence and guarantees His faithfulness by continuing to honor His word. This will give you comfort and strength.

Remember the word unto thy servant, upon which thou hast caused me to hope. This *is* my comfort in my affliction: for thy word hath quickened me ...

For as the rain cometh down, and the snow from heaven, and returneth not thither, but watereth the earth, and maketh it bring forth and bud, that it may give seed to the sower, and bread to the eater: So shall my word be that goeth forth out of my mouth: it shall not return unto me void, but it shall accomplish that which I please, and it shall prosper *in the thing* whereto I sent it. For ye shall go out with joy, and be led forth with peace: the mountains and the hills shall break forth before you into singing, and all the trees of the field shall clap *their* hands (Ps. 119:49–50, Isa. 55:10–12 KJV).

You have to come to grips with the fact that there is no substitute for God's Word when you are hurting; when you are hurting, God will always send His Word. He has sent His Word to heal us. You will find your strength in God's Word.

9. ***You must repent in the areas where your own sin caused the damage.***

I know that there may have been a lot of people who hurt you in your life's journey. But you have to repent of the things you did that put you in the position to be hurt. It's easy to say that they did this and they did that, but do an honest self-evaluation and see what part you may have played to entice the trauma and change your character in that area.

Pay attention to the choices you make. You are responsible for the things you do. For example, if you're not ready or you are unsure about a situation and knew it was a bad choice but let your friends convince you that it was the right thing to do, that's on you. Discipline yourself not to be influenced by others when you're unsure of something. Or you may have a bad habit or a strong desire to do unhealthy things that are temporarily gratifying but that make you vulnerable to being hurt and abused. Discontinue practicing it, and change your thinking. *Repent* in that area; *stop doing it!*

10. *This is spiritual* **warfare!**

Ephesians 6:10–17 describes this war that we all are involved in against God's enemy and the enemy's troops. The human race is actually wrestling with demonic forces in the atmosphere that are opposing, oppressing, or possessing people.

> This is no afternoon athletic contest that we'll walk away from and forget about in a couple of hours. This is for keeps, a life-or-death fight to the finish against the Devil and all his angels (*demons*) (Eph. 6:12 TM emphasis mine).

The people who came against you most likely were being coerced or driven by a demonic spirit. The devil employed a weak person who did not want to get help. There is a real devil who's behind the *pain* and disturbance in the world and your life too!

This war also consists of what goes on in your mind. The mind is the management center of your spirit, soul, and body and is where the actual spiritual battle is joined and fought. The mind is the battlefield, and the world we live in is the battleground that the spiritual war is played out on.

> For though we walk in the flesh, we do not war after the flesh: (For the weapons of our warfare *are* not carnal (of human origin), but mighty through God to the pulling down of strong holds) *Casting down imaginations*, and every high thing that exalteth itself against the knowledge of God, and bringing into captivity every *thought* to the obedience of Christ; And having in a readiness to revenge all disobedience, when your obedience is fulfilled (2 Cor. 10:3–6 KJV, emphasis mine).

Therefore, you need to persevere and grow in the Lord that you may stand against the tricks of the devil and become a vessel God uses to deliver others who wrestle with the same issues you've overcome. Learn to deal with your pain so you can do your part to stop the cycle in your family and the world.

> Wherefore seeing we also are compassed about with so great a cloud of witnesses, let us lay aside every weight,

and the sin which doth so easily beset *us*, and let us run with patience the race that is set before us, Looking unto Jesus the author and finisher of *our* faith; who for the joy that was set before him endured the cross, despising the shame, and is set down at the right hand of the throne of God. For consider him that endured such contradiction of sinners against himself, lest ye be wearied and faint in your minds (Heb. 12:1–3 KJV).

God has so much for you to do and tremendous blessings for you too! Don't let the past or your pain prevent it. Look to Jesus, who is the author and finisher of your faith. Consider the contradiction of people He went through and came out victoriously for you so that you won't get wearied and give up. *Jesus **loves** you and had you in His heart when **He hung on the cross.***

Nay, in all these things we are more than conquerors through him that loved us. For I am persuaded, that neither death, nor life, nor angels, nor principalities, nor powers, nor things present, nor things to come, Nor height, nor depth, nor any other creature, shall be able to separate us from the love of God, which is in Christ Jesus our Lord. Romans 8:37-39 (KJV)

CHAPTER NINE ✠

THE BREAKING POINT

There are individual and corporate moments in which a condition or situation becomes critical. Most people have to come to the end of themselves before getting extremely persistent about change. Are you sick and tired of being sick and tired of your circumstances? Some of you reading this book are tired of doing the same thing over and over and over again and getting the same unproductive results. There are some people who are in and out of jail just like a rubber band snaps back to its previous position every time you let it go. Or maybe you feel like there is something missing in your life and it has been like that for a very long time, and you've attempted to find the missing link but can't.

Now that you have a better understanding of how present curses and their consequences are, you should be ready to make sure that you are freed from being the victim of any—directly or indirectly!

We've already learned (and this may seem foolish to the headstrong scholarly or uneducated thinker) that this earth is cursed from the fall of the first humans (Gen. 3:14, 17–18). Ever since that time, there has been a variety of pain, suffering, greed, and grief comparable to the wound that was incurred upon Adam and Eve when they realized they were separated from God, and the first murder was between their children. Like the wound that was incurred upon King David and his daughter Tamar, who was raped by her brother; and her other brother murdered the one who raped her (2 Samuel 13:1-29). From day to day, year to year, and century to century, lives have been packed with trauma that could and can be prevented in most cases. I say "most cases" because there will always be people who will choose to stay in the condition they're in because they enjoy being morally wrong. But there comes a point when you must realize and face the truth that the cycle has to be broken in your life, your family's life, and your relationships!

God knew that you would desire to come out of this oppression, and He also didn't want you in it in the first place. Again, I need to say that God loved us so much that He gave us a mind to think for ourselves. Therefore, the choices that people make will affect another person for better or worse. That's what we've encountered from the wrong choice of Adam and Eve. And even if they had done the right thing, someone else would have eaten from the tree of the knowledge of evil and we still would be in the situation that society is in at this present time. Adam and Eve's choice has affected humanity for the worse. What's more, God didn't want us to wrestle and be victimized by curses anyway. Nevertheless, because of the gift of freedom of choice, numerous people continue to allow the cursed cycle that was brought on us by our ancestors to run rampant. However, God knew about you before He even created the world. He prepared in His heart a way for you to come out of and rule over the *curse*, its pain, and its consequences.

> It cost God plenty to get you out of that dead-end, empty-headed life you grew up in. He paid with Christ's sacred blood, you know. He died like an unblemished, sacrificial lamb. And this was no afterthought. Even though it has only lately—at the end of the ages—become public knowledge, God always knew he was going to do this for you (1 Peter 1:18–20 TM).

Jesus Christ actually became your substitute by becoming a curse for you.

> Christ redeemed us from that self-defeating, [cursed] life by absorbing it completely into himself. Do you remember the Scripture that says, "Cursed is everyone who hangs on a tree"? That is what happened when Jesus was nailed to the Cross: He became a [curse], and at the same time dissolved the [curse] (Gal. 3:13 TM emphasis mine).

Hopefully, now you understand that Jesus became a curse for you and that He came to set the captives free. You've persevered or are in the process of getting to the root of your wound by following the ten principles in the previous chapter; now let's move on through the breaking point.

The Power of a Made-Up Mind

The mind is an awesome piece of machinery, so to speak. It is the seat of reflective consciousness comprising the faculties of perceiving and understanding, and those of judging and determining.[1] The mind reflects on circumstances it perceives and allows you to determine how they affect you. This dynamic volition gives a person understanding on what to do in regard to the goal he or she desires. Some goals are ignorantly destructive, and some are healthy and beneficial. When the information of absolute truth enters the mind, the insight will help to determine the healthy goal that should be set and achieved. *In this case, we're not only talking about breaking out of the curse but staying out!*

Once a person has uncompromisingly made up his or her mind to do something, it is difficult to change it. Determination sets in like an incurable disease. For example, if you were getting ready to walk across a street and someone screamed at you, "Watch out, there is a car coming!" the insight that is gained from the entering of an absolute truth (you're about to get run over by a car) would cause you to "make up your mind" that you're not going to cross that street. From the determination of a "made-up mind," no friend, foe, or loved one can talk or coerce you into crossing that street while the car is coming. You're just not going to do it because you understand the consequences.

That should be the mental tenacity you apply to changing your life. Every success ever made or achieved has come about as a result of a decision made at some point. Making real decisions is a habit that must be cultivated if you want to succeed in life. Many people think that when they wish for something, they have made a decision. Another example is when someone says, "I want to stop smoking." This is an expression of a wish, and a wish does not have the dynamic power of a made-up mind! The decision of a made-up mind is something that's fixed; something that may be termed as irrevocable. When you make a real decision, you draw a line. You burn your ships and destroy every possibility of a retreat. You leave yourself with no option but to succeed. The decision of a made-up mind fuels the burning desire to accomplish something and will give you the control to manage other vital decisions, in addition to obtaining the end result of having power over the things that have victimized you.

---

1   *Vine's Expository Dictionary.*

You can achieve anything you really want in life if you are ready to make the decision to achieve it. Once your mind is made up, whatever you desire is what you get. *A desire for freedom brings freedom.*

You must be aware that if you do not "make up your mind" to change your life today, no one will change it for you. You must be ready to change and bring that change into effect by constantly practicing what you have decided for. Be persistent! When you have a made-up mind about your life and Jesus Christ, you attune yourself to tremendous extra power because of the provisions Almighty God has made for you and available to you.

As Dr. Martin Luther King so eloquently stated, *"A mind is a terrible thing to waste."*

The Power of a Changed Mind

Now that you have made the decision to have a "made-up mind," the next step is to renew your mind.

If you change the way you think, you can change the way you live. In other words, you have to learn how to view your life and the world you live in from the perspective that God has established. The most important step you must take is the reality of the spiritual world and how it corresponds with this natural world; the vital move to spirituality. To move from those things that are without the spirit to the things that involve the Spirit of God.

> And be not drunk with wine, wherein is excess; but be filled with the Spirit … (Eph. 5:18 KJV).

The Holy Spirit is the author of the Word of God, the teacher of the Word of God, and the power of the Word of God. It is only through His presence that any person can understand God's Word.

> But the anointing which ye have received of him abideth in you, and ye need not that any man teach you: but as the same anointing teacheth you of all things, and is truth, and is no lie, and even as it hath taught you, ye shall abide in him (1 John 2:27 KJV).

This passage of Scripture is not saying that you don't need anyone else to teach you. But it is referring to the Holy Spirit dwelling inside of the believer. He will bear witness to the truth when He hears it because He's living inside of you. In other words, you will know the truth of God's Word when you hear it if it's being correctly preached, studied, or taught.

It is the process of the anointing of God's Holy Spirit that will open your understanding to the things of God and will grow a changed mind in you as you do your part.

> Study to shew thyself approved unto God, a workman that needeth not to be ashamed, rightly dividing the word of truth. (2 Timothy 2:15 KJV)

You will begin to perceive and understand spiritual things that may seem foolish to society. But don't worry, you're not crazy!

> But the natural (unsaved) man receiveth not the things of the Spirit of God: for they are foolishness unto him: neither can he know *them*, because they are spiritually discerned (1 Cor. 2:14 KJV, emphasis mine).

So God instructs us to come to Him with willingness, an open heart, and a teachable spirit so He can fill us with Himself and give us the proper insight about life.

> I plead with you therefore, brethren, by the compassions of God, to present all your [*faculties*] to Him as a living and holy sacrifice acceptable to Him. This with you will be an act of reasonable worship. And do not follow the customs of the present age (society that ignores God), but be transformed by the entire [*renewal*] of your [*minds*], so that you may learn by experience what God's will is—that will which is good and beautiful and perfect (Rom. 12:1–2 Weymouth New Testament, emphasis mine).

When the apostle Paul, who wrote these passages of Scripture, was preaching this message, it was a time during the rule of the Roman Empire. This was a nation that dominated the world at one time, and idol worship was rampant in that society. Idols were the norm for many of their citizens because it had become a national tradition. This world empire was also executing Christians and there were a lot of them who endured brutal persecution. Moreover, it was the believer in Christ Paul was telling to present their faculties to God as a living sacrifice and to be transformed by a *renewed mind*. Because of the persecution, it was a challenge for them to change how they viewed their present reality and declare that they had to see reality the way Christ wanted them to see it while in the face of brutal and often-fatal opposition.

How the Roman Empire relates to our society today is that many American citizens are not concerned at all about God and His design for life. Their thought life is a symbol and pattern of flat-out idolatry. It is easily seen by the rebellion they exhibit in their behavior. Therefore it is a challenge for those who have a made-up mind to change their view of reality to where God wants it to be—to change their view to a place where God wants them to see, to a place where God wants them to hear, and to a condition of how He wants them to live.

However, there is a powerful transition that occurs when you enter into an authentic relationship with Christ. You begin to spend time in the Word and under the Word, and within time your focus on life is different. God's thoughts become your thoughts and a point of reference that helps you to determine choices; when your mind changes, your perspective changes. When your mind changes, you will move from being a hurter to being a helper; when your mind changes, you will move from being a spectator to a participator; when your mind changes, you will move from being hopeless to hopeful!

What God is really after is your mind. He wants it out of the low place of deception, the low place of spiritual ignorance, the low place of a tunnel vision, depression, discouragement, the curse, and doubting! *God can't take you to another level in life unless you take your mind with you.*

> But ye have not so learned Christ; If so be that ye have heard him, and have been taught by him, as the truth is in Jesus: That ye put off concerning the former conversation (behavior) the old man, which is corrupt according to the deceitful lusts; *And be renewed in the spirit of your mind ...* (Eph. 4:20–23 KJV, emphasis mine).

When you begin to comprehend the power of a changed mind according to God's design, you can understand how to tap into everything God has for your life. There are four vital things to know about God's blueprint and development for a changed mind. *The first is to know that as long as you are alive on this earth, you should never get to a point where you think you've arrived and there's no more room to grow.* Walking with God is a lifelong process.

For if a man think himself to be something, when he is nothing, he deceiveth himself (Gal. 6:3 KJV).

The second vital thing is to spend time in God's Word every day.

Study to shew thyself approved unto God, a workman that needeth not to be ashamed, rightly dividing the word of truth (2 Tim. 2:15 KJV).

The study of God's Word is your spiritual food: just as your body will starve from malnutrition if you don't feed it, so will your spirit if you don't feed it God's Word.

But he answered and said, it is written, Man shall not live by bread alone, *but by every word that proceedeth out of the mouth of God* (Matthew 4:4 KJV emphasis mine).

The third vital thing is to make sure you're being properly taught so you can see life from a biblical perspective instead of a worldly religious perspective. Find yourself a pastor or teacher who's leading a church that is a living example of God's purpose on earth.

And he gave some, apostles; and some, prophets; and some, evangelists; and some, pastors and teachers; For the perfecting of the saints, for the work of the ministry, for the edifying of the body of Christ (Eph. 4:11–12 KJV).

The fourth and final vital thing is to put into action the Word of God that you have put into your heart.

But be ye doers of the word, and not hearers only, deceiving (fooling) your own selves. For if any be a hearer of the word, and not a doer, he is like unto a man beholding his natural face in a glass (a mirror): For he beholdeth himself, and goeth his way, and straightway forgetteth what manner of man he was. But whoso looketh into the perfect law of liberty, and continueth *therein*, he being not a forgetful hearer, *but a doer of the work*, this man shall be blessed in his deed (what he or she does) (James 1:22–25 KJV, emphasis mine).

A word is a medium by which thoughts are expressed; therefore the Bible is the mind of God on a printed page that He has given us to renew our thinking. As you feed yourself on the Word of God and absorb it into your heart, you will nurture a *made-up mind* into a *"renewed mind"* and experience the power of a *"changed mind"*!

> And the Word was made flesh, and dwelt among us ...
> (John 1:14 KJV).

This passage of Scripture is referring to Jesus, who is the "Word of God" and walked the face of this earth. But He also left you an inheritance so you can carry on where He left off when you have made up your mind to follow Christ. That's who you are in Christ too: *the word made flesh. The power of a changed mind* will take you to your next level of spiritual maturity.

CHAPTER TEN

FASTING

The word "fasting" means to abstain. When it comes to spiritual things, there are several important benefits of fasting. One is to break immoral routines (wicked lifestyles); another is to help grow out of or abstain from selfishness. There are more benefits of fasting, but our focus is breaking the curse and maintaining freedom. Fasting will help you mature in self-control, honoring people you come into contact with in life with fairness and honesty, not with wickedness, heavy burdens, and oppression.

> *Is* not this the fast that I have chosen? to loose the bands of wickedness, to undo the heavy burdens, and to let the oppressed go free, and that ye break every yoke? *Is it* not to deal thy bread to the hungry, and that thou bring the poor that are cast out to thy house? when thou seest the naked, that thou cover him; and that thou hide not thyself from thine own flesh? (Isaiah 58:6, 7 KJV)

Fasting is to help people break loose from various personal vices so that they won't treat others out of anger, revenge, or resentment from an unhealed wounded heart; and most of all, to stop self-destruction. It's called freedom! And again I want to say that it helps to gain self-control. Remember, we've talked about how hurt people, hurt people.

The word "wickedness" in this verse is a little deeper than sin. Wickedness is a lifestyle where sin has so set in that it has begun to develop character. Sin cannot in and of itself develop character. But the continual practice of sin will increase into a habit that eventually becomes part of a person's character. Remember, we learned this process in chapter seven when looking at how bad habits are formed.

Verse seven teaches us how to abstain from being greedy or stingy with things you have that someone else may need for survival. If you are a person who may have trouble turning these necessities loose, fasting will also help you share your personal possessions with those who are in need, which is what Kingdom work consists of. Practicing these virtues while you yourself are abstaining from your natural food frees you from selfish selfishness.

When the discipline of fasting coupled with the obedience of sharing and helping the needy becomes part of your natural character, it helps purify your perception of God's communication and presence. When you live out these things, God says, **then**:

> My favor will shine on you like the morning sun, and your [wounds] will be quickly *healed*. I will always be with you to save you; my presence will protect you on every side. *When you pray, I will answer you. When you call to me, I will respond* (Isa. 58:8–9, TEV emphasis mine).

Fasting will not only be a major part in the equation of your freedom from certain bondages, but you will also be in an effective position to help others who are struggling with the same oppression that you've been delivered from.

When your life is in tune or at one with God, you are then able to be an effective soldier in God's army by doing your part for the Kingdom of God on earth. Let's look at some of the other reasons for fasting in the Old Testament after a person has personally gotten him or herself in line with God. They fasted when;

1. In war or at the threat of warfare (Judg. 20:26).
2. In Times when loved ones were sick (2 Sam. 12:16–23).
3. When a loved one died (1 Sam. 31:13).
4. When they sought God's forgiveness (Deut. 9:15–18).
5. When faced with impending danger (2 Chron. 20:3).
6. To get direct instructions from God (2 Chron. 20:14–19).
7. To "humble" themselves before the Lord (Ps. 35:13).

How the physical war at that time corresponds with this day and time is that you are in a spiritual war against self, Satan, his demons, and the world-system (a society that ignores God).

But the fasting we're discussing in this chapter is for the purpose of breaking strongholds that have kept you bound to curses, bad habits, and addictions. The disciples of Jesus encountered a problem where only prayer and fasting could change the situation back to normal. A man's son was considered to be a lunatic (mentally deranged), which can be compared to the mental disposition of a severe alcoholic, drug addict, or depressed person in our day and time.

> And when they were come to the multitude, there came to him a *certain* man, kneeling down to him, and saying, Lord, have mercy on my son: for he is lunatick, and sore vexed: for ofttimes he falleth into the fire, and oft into the water.
>
> *And I brought him to thy disciples, and they could not cure him...*
>
> ... And Jesus rebuked the devil; and he departed out of him: and the child was cured from that very hour.
>
> Then came the disciples to Jesus apart, and said, Why could not we cast him out? And Jesus said unto them... *Howbeit this kind goeth not out but by prayer and fasting* (Matt. 17:14–16, 18–21 KJV, emphasis mine).

The disciplines we have been discussing in the previous chapters, along with fasting, when coupled with prayer and the Holy Spirit, empower you to overcome any bad habits, addictions, and curses. Determining if you should fast or not depends on how severe the grip of bondage is on you.

There are physically bad habits and addictions some people have for which there is no miracle cure. What I mean is that there is not anything that goes "Zap" because you prayed and then all of a sudden you are healed! *It takes work on your part.* And when you spend time in prayer and abstain from food for a period of time, you gain inner strength from the Holy Spirit in an unusual way that gives you power over that oppression for the time being. Eventually a person gains inner strength by the Holy Spirit to rule over that *addictive* habit if they persevere. We've already noted that the human being is a creature of habit. With the help of the Holy Spirit and the application of godly principles we've discussed, a person can transform any bad habit, addiction, or curse into a lifestyle of discipline that consists of good habits that overrule the bad ones. There may have to be a series of prayer and fasting at set periods of time to inevitably overcome the oppression. *Or there may have to be a period of time for detox if the habit is substance abuse or alcohol.* It just depends on how severe the stronghold is and what habit you're dealing with. There are different kinds of addictions and bad habits, and some may have a stronger grip or obsession than others.

We've already learned that a very important purpose of fasting is that it will enable you to perceive God *communicating* to you. It is a good discipline when waiting and wanting to hear from God. Hearing from the Lord usually happens one of four ways or in any combination of the four:

1. From the Word of God (reading the Bible).
2. By the indwelling of the Holy Spirit (an inner confirmation).
3. Through the words of another anointed person (the sermon at church).
4. And/or circumstances (Prov. 3:6).

Of course, every one of these four ways must be in line with the Bible. God will never, ever contradict His written Word. *Remember, the Bible is the mind of God on a printed page*

There are some people who consider fasting unnecessary and undesirable, and a lot of people just ignore it all together. Then there are some people who just don't know how to fast. However, Jesus said we should fast.

> Then came to him (Jesus) the disciples of John, saying, why do we and the Pharisees fast oft, but thy disciples fast not? And Jesus said unto them, Can the children of the bride chamber mourn, as long as the bridegroom is with them? but the days will come, when the bridegroom (Jesus) shall be taken from them, *and then shall they fast* (Matt. 9:14–15 KJV, emphasis mine).

Personal fasting is also to be done in private, between you and God only. It is not to be done in front of others with an attempt of making yourself look spiritual or holy.

Moreover when ye fast, be not, as the hypocrites, of a sad countenance: for they disfigure their faces, that they may appear unto men to fast. Verily I say unto you, they have their reward.

But thou, when thou fastest, anoint thine head, and wash thy face;

That thou appear not unto men to fast, but unto thy Father which is in secret: *and thy Father, which seeth in secret, shall reward thee openly* (Matt. 6:16–18 KJV).

The truth is that properly fasting is a necessary discipline. Pastor Eddie Whitelaw of the Unity Temple Church of God in Christ in Jackson, Tennessee, has a saying that goes, "If you don't pray, you won't stay, and if you don't fast, you won't last." In other words, fasting may be vital to getting out and staying out of the condition that's negatively affecting your life.

Fasting is spiritual, and it affects the soul. It is a healing process for a soul that has been infected with unclean spirits, bad habits, addictions, and dominating curses. It is a sure way of confronting the infection and driving it out of your life. When you understand what you're after in the spirit, it makes it easier to go without food in the natural. Fasting therefore is for a purpose; the purpose of hearing from God, spiritual and physical deliverance, and cleansing of your soul. When a person fasts, he or she is seeking the favor of God, His divine intervention, spiritual and emotional healing, or the ability and the authority to move forward with confidence in a given situation.

Again I want to say that there are other reasons and benefits of fasting, but people must do their part in getting themselves in order before they can be effective in helping others or participating in corporate fasting. The other thing to note is that it is not a good idea to fast just because it's something spiritual to do. Don't do it because it sounds like a good thing to do! *Take fasting seriously!*

A person can go without eating and it will profit him or her nothing if it is not correctly done and/or taken seriously. You will just have starved yourself for a period of time, and the hunger pains will be your only reward. Fasting is more than just not eating; it is a spiritual encounter with God. It is to be done only when the occasion is serious. There are some things that you don't have to fast over, they are just common sense. That's one reason God gave us a mind to think for ourselves. You have to understand that you fast when you desperately desire God's help—when you need God's help for things that are beyond your control, when it seems like nothing you're doing is working.

Here are some important instructions for personal fasting:

1. If you've never fasted before, start slow, fasting for only brief periods of time. Don't hurt yourself by attempting to go a long period of time without food if you've never done this before. You will probably fail; you have to learn how to fast gradually. Also learn to end your fast slow, and learn to slowly break your fast with fruits and vegetables in small amounts. Don't break a fast with a large full-course meal because it is not healthy to strain your digestive system all of a sudden when it has been in a relaxed condition for a period of time.

2. Fast when you have time to spend in prayerful meditation. When you fast, you have to carve out time for meditation and prayer. You can't fully benefit from fasting if you don't take out a period of time during the day to shut down everything and spend time praying, meditating, and seeking God. Fasting has to have prayer alongside it in order for it to be effective. You have to be in communication with God.

3. You also have to humble yourself in God's sight when you are fasting. You have to go to God in humility. One thing a fast is designed to do is to bring you into humility.

4. Then, what is very significant is that you must seek a favorable answer while in prayer for God's will to be made known to you. Be sure to ask God for what you desire, but be ready to accept His will, whatever it is. He knows what is best for you and the best way to accomplish it even when it doesn't make sense to you.

Did you know that there are a lot of things that keep people from fasting? I want to share these things with you because I don't want them to keep you from the blessings and benefits of a fast.

1. Ignorance! Countless people will not fast because they don't know the facts about it. They will complain because going without eating seems foolish to them.

2. Selfishness will keep a person from fasting. That's because some people will esteem food higher than doing God's will. They may act like they are participating in a fast but sneak off to eat a meal. You too have to be careful not to try to sneak in a little snack while fasting, thinking that God will understand.

3. Another reason is indifference. A lot of people don't see the need to fast so they don't even attempt to do it when in certain spiritual struggles. They try to overcome by their own fleshly strength and volition. This can be dangerous when there is a need for a corporate fast of the church because this particular person will not participate when the whole congregation is seeking a breakthrough. One or two people can mess up the entire fast and cause defeat.

4. The lack of self-control; people will not fast because the lack of self-control when it comes to the craving for food. They will not deny themselves of that pleasure just for a short season of time to gain deliverance. The Scripture says:

> And when he (Jesus) had called the people *unto him* with his disciples also, he said unto them, whosoever will come after me, *let him deny himself, and take up his cross, and follow me* (Mark 8:34 KJV, emphasis mine).

People have to deny themselves of the pleasure of eating food when it comes to fasting. And there are other things that seem pleasurable to hold on to in the natural when it comes to serving God. But spiritually, they can spell disaster in a person's life. Look what the next verses say about the people who lack self control and seek to do things out of their own strength, their own way, and their own ability.

> For whosoever will save his life shall lose it; but whosoever shall lose his life for my sake and the gospel's, the same shall save it. *For what shall it profit a man, if he shall gain the whole world, and lose his own soul?* (Mark 8: 35–36 KJV, emphasis mine).

People will attempt to hold onto to stuff thinking they will keep it or save it but they will ultimately lose it; even their soul will be lost or defeated because it has been contaminated with bad habits, addictions, and curses that can't be permanently broken. What they are trying to keep materially, what they are trying to do their own way spiritually, out of ignorance, they will lose, even their very life, because they have chosen to value things that are ungodly and of the world system above the disciplines of God. They have chosen to put their selfish actions and appetites above God, who is the only deliverer of a person's soul!

When you learn how to obey the disciplines that God requires and learn how to release the things you have been falsely taught to hold on to by a society that ignores God, that doesn't know God, then you will actually save it and end up with more than you started with. Boy! That includes your very life! This is a very important foundational principal in the things of God that you don't want to miss. God says that the very thing you're trying to hold on to you will lose, but if you let it go for His sake you save it and end up with more than you started.

5. Then there are people with the wrong priorities. They just want to place the good and the pleasant above that which is spiritual. Basically, all they want is the good things and not to do the work that is involved in accomplishing the spiritual.

6. Also, there are those who have the false conception about Christianity. They just don't understand what it means to be a disciplined follower of Jesus Christ. Disciples of God are disciplined people.

Once again, I want to remind you that the moment you begin to deny your flesh of its natural desire, it will cause you to be more in tune to hear the voice of the Lord. There is no doubt about it; the very moment you deny your flesh you are moving into a spiritual dimension where you're going to discern God's voice. The Word of God will be so clear to you that you will hear revelation, insight, and instruction. It's not that your pastor is preaching any better, but through fasting you have prepared yourself to receive better. Deuteronomy 9:18–25 is a very good example of this.

Fasting can also place you in a realm more easily prone to the attack of the devil. You are in a condition and position of spiritual communication and the enemy doesn't want you to get what you're after because you are a threat to his kingdom and plans.

> The thief (Satan) cometh not, but for to steal, and to kill, and to destroy: I am (Jesus) come that they might have life, and that they might have *it* more abundantly. (John 10:10 KJV, emphasis mine)

CHAPTER ELEVEN

BLESSINGS

The more than life that is the abundant life that Jesus gives us is nothing short of a blessing (John 10:10b). Blessings are the total opposite of curses. A blessing means the form of words used in invoking the bestowal of good instead of evil. To invoke is to speak audibly, and we've already learned how God "spoke" this world into existence. He spoke and creation came into physical reality. We can actually see, taste, touch, and smell what He spoke. He said and it was so, and what we're living in right now is the continuation of the "so" that He said.

> For as the rain cometh down, and the snow from heaven, and returneth not thither, but watereth the earth, and maketh it bring forth and bud, that it may give seed to the sower, and bread to the eater:
>
> So shall my word be that goeth forth out of my mouth: *it shall not return unto me void, but it shall accomplish that which I please, and it shall prosper in the thing whereto I sent it* (Isa. 55:10–11 KJV emphasis mine).

God has spoken tremendous blessings over the life of every human being on the face of this earth, but they can only be fully experienced and realized to those who are born-again believers in Jesus Christ. The whole physical earth was created to be a blessing for us, but because of sin there has been death, decay, and destruction. Even the creation itself is groaning in pain.

> For we know that the whole creation groaneth and travaileth in pain together until now (Rom. 8:22 KJV).

The "until now" in this verse signifies that it is high time for you to take your position in Christ and start living in the *blessed* purpose that God has designed for you so Heaven can be experienced on earth. We can't change the world, but if you submit to the Lordship of Jesus Christ and do your part, the world will fall into its appointed place, because Christ has already overcome the world (John 16:33).

Remember, we've learned that the meaning of "spiritual" consists of the unseen human thoughts, emotions, and desires, as well as the celestial spirits and the invisible world where all of the activity of spiritual reality takes place.

> For by him were all things created, that are in heaven, and that are in earth, [*visible* and *invisible*], whether *they be* thrones, or dominions, or principalities, or powers: all things were created by him, and for him: (Col 1:16 KJV emphasis mine)

Consider what this verse is saying.

(a) Thrones: are positions of power and authority.

(b) Dominions: To rule over territories.

(c) Principalities: Spirit beings, either angelic or demonic, which have rulership.

(d) Powers: The powers that principalities or spiritual leaders wield.

Not only were these positions and things created by Christ, but they were also created for Christ. This is so that God (who is love) can bless us through Christ. It is through Christ we have spiritual authority. This inheritance has all spiritual blessings in heavenly places.

> Blessed *be* the God and Father of our Lord Jesus Christ, who hath blessed us with all spiritual blessings in heavenly *places* in Christ: (Ephesians 1:3 KJV)

Now that we understand that the spiritual dimension consists of the thoughts, emotions, and realm where spirits dwell, the heavenly place in this verse is the position in an authentic spiritual (invisible) city that's in the atmosphere, and only those who are born again can experience the assets of it. Those with the mental disposition of the new birth actually live there with Christ while physically present here on earth. *Spiritually we have been supernaturally transferred into God's Kingdom.*

> Giving thanks unto the Father, which hath made us meet to be partakers of the inheritance of the saints in light: Who hath delivered us from the power of darkness, and hath [translated] *us* into the [kingdom] of his dear Son.

> ...You've come to Mount Zion, the city where the living God resides. The [invisible] Jerusalem is populated by *throngs of festive angels* and [*Christian citizens*]. It is the city where God is Judge, with judgments that make us just.

> You've come to Jesus, who presents us with a new covenant, a fresh charter from God. He is the Mediator of this covenant. The murder of Jesus, unlike Abel's—a homicide that cried out for vengeance—became a proclamation of grace.

> Now therefore ye are no more [strangers] and [foreigners], but [fellowcitizens] with the saints, and of the [household of God]; And are built upon the foundation of the apostles and prophets, Jesus Christ himself being the chief corner *stone*;

> In whom all the building fitly framed together groweth unto an *holy temple in the Lord*:

> *In whom ye also are builded together for an habitation of God through the Spirit* (Col. 1:12–13 KJV; Heb. 12:22–24 TM; Eph. 2:19–22 KJV emphasis mine).

After Jesus Christ's resurrection, He proclaimed that all power in heaven (the atmosphere) and earth (physical land) is given unto Him.

> And Jesus came and spake unto them, saying, All power is given unto me in heaven and in earth (Matt. 28:18 KJV).

The night before His crucifixion, He prayed that you would have the position of all power in heaven and earth along with Him:

> Neither [pray] I for these alone, but for them also which shall believe on me through their word;

> That they all may be one; as thou, Father, *art* in me, and I in thee, that they also may be one in us: that the world may believe that thou hast sent me.
>
> And the [*glory*] which thou gavest me I have given them; *that they may be one, even as we are one*:
>
> I in them, and thou in me, that they may be made perfect in one; and that the world may know that thou hast sent me, and hast loved them, as thou hast loved me.
>
> *Father, I will that they also, whom thou hast given me, be with me where I am*; that they may behold my glory, which thou hast given me: for thou lovedst me before the foundation of the world. (John 17:20-24 KJV emphasis mine)

So what is all of this saying to us? It is saying that God has spoken, prepared, and executed an inheritance (blessing) over your life that has put you in an authoritative position, including citizenship in His Kingdom through Jesus Christ! In this position are all power, all authority, and all strength to overcome bad habits, addictions, and curses. He's practically saying that He has blessed you to be one with Him. God is living in your body (His temple) through the indwelling of His Holy Spirit in you. This understanding is something to cheer and scream about because it discloses who you really are—your true identity. You're not an addict, gang banger, prostitute, extortioner, or whatever! You're a child of the living God, and to top it off, this opportunity was made available to you before you knew you!

> He hath chosen us [in him] before the foundation of the world, that we should be holy and without blame before him in love: Having [predestinated] us unto the adoption of children by Jesus Christ to himself, *according to the good pleasure of his will*, To the praise of the glory of his grace, wherein he hath *made us accepted in the beloved* (Eph.1:4–6 KJV, emphasis mine).

You do not have to continue to be the cursed child, the addict, or the person who's stuck in a bad lifestyle. You are somebody with godly significance who can make a difference in your own life, your family, your church, and your community.

The power of God that is made available for you and to you to overcome your circumstance is the same power of the Holy Spirit that moved upon the face of the earth at creation (Gen. 1:1). It is the same power that was available to Moses when the Red Sea was parted, and it is the same power that raised Jesus Christ from the dead (Exod. 14:21–22; Mark 16:6).

The apostle Paul prayed that you will get the knowledge and wisdom of this inheritance.

> Making mention of you in my prayers;
>
> That the God of our Lord Jesus Christ, the Father of glory, may give unto you the spirit of *wisdom* and *revelation* in the knowledge of him:
>
> The eyes of your understanding being enlightened; that ye may [know] what is the hope of his calling, and what the [*riches of the glory of his inheritance in the saints*],
>
> *And what is the exceeding greatness of his power to us-ward who believe, according to the working of his mighty power, Which he wrought in Christ, when he raised him from the dead, and set him at his own right hand in the heavenly places,*
>
> Far above all principality, and power, and might, and dominion, and every name that is named, not only in this world, but also in that which is to come:
>
> And hath put all things under his feet, and gave him to be the head over all things to the church, Which is his body, the fullness of him that filleth all in all (Eph. 1:16–23 KJV emphasis mine).

This is an extremely thought-provoking understanding for some people and an awesome revelation for others. The apostle Paul says that God has "put" all things under the feet of Jesus, and if you belong to Jesus Christ, you're part of His body and are in this position as a coworker with Christ!

Listen! The problems you may be having with your family are under His feet!

The problems in your career are under His feet!

The corruption all around you is under His feet!

Jesus Christ is the sum total of the whole equation of life with all things under His authority, and God has made provision for you to prevail in spite of your circumstance.

> Nay, in all these things we are more than [*conquerors*] through him that loved us.
>
> For I am persuaded, that neither death, nor life, nor angels, nor principalities, nor powers, nor things present, nor things to come,
>
> Nor height, nor depth, nor any other creature, shall be able to separate us from the [*love of God*], [*which is in Christ Jesus our Lord*] (Rom. 8:37–39 KJV, emphasis mine).

You are somebody, your life has significance, you were created with and for a purpose, and most of all, *you are loved and blessed by God!*

A DREAM

Where there is no [vision] the people perish ...
—Proverbs 29:18

To realize the depth of love God has for you is one of the most profound discoveries a person can experience. The Bible compares being a citizen of God's Kingdom to a person who has found a hidden treasure and focuses all of his life in the pursuit of purpose by laying aside the habits, people, places, and things that are dream killers (Matt. 13:44–52).

Please remember that God is not going to tell you do to something that He's not going to do! So if His commandment is to love Him with all of your heart, mind, soul, and strength, then realizing that He already loves you with all of His heart, His mind, His soul, and His strength should turn your heart toward Him and strengthen your confidence in hope (Matt. 22:37). This whole universe was in the heart and mind of God when He created it, and to this day we cannot even fathom how some of it functions. But His Love for you, me, and the human race came out of that same mind—a mind that's infinite. There is no end to it; the depth of it is forever long, deep, wide, and high! Man, that's a lot of *love!*

Sheltered in the idea of the Creator's love you were designed in His image (Gen. 1:26). In other words, you were created with an invisible entity (your spirit and soul) that has an innate ability to function with the same emotional and expressive attributes as God, including the power of creativity and imagination. In your heart of hearts, there is a passion to accomplish something that you've always dreamed of.

The desires of these passions are part of your God-given instructions that pertain to your purpose. Passion coupled with the idea of bringing it into reality is what vision is. When a person really discovers the realism of this and begins to implement it in harmony with an active personal relationship with Jesus Christ, it energizes and vitalizes him or her. It plays a significant part in nurturing your inner desire of wondering why you are here on earth. It also helps you to stay focused and to make the right choices in life even when something else that's good comes along that may not be in the best interest or in the direction of your purpose. Understanding vision and realizing its purpose helps you to stay on course.

The word "perish" in Proverbs 29:18 implies unproductiveness and ineffectiveness in life, with the possible end result being a premature death. Depending on the ungodly way of life, the premature death can be violent.

Perishing is when someone is living an intimate lifestyle with dream-killers that have blocked or put out the light of their vision. They're working hard, sweating hard, but making no real progress in life. They're not going anywhere. Our world is filled with people who are busy but not ultimately effective or satisfied. They are doing much, expending time and energy, but getting little of value accomplished. Consequently, they spend their lives toiling away but never making any headway with contentment, peace, and purpose. Dream killers can be:

1. An ungodly lifestyle that keeps you from reaching or even maximizing your potential.
2. Negative people.
3. Laziness and procrastination.

Looking at these three categories, the first is an ungodly lifestyle. If you've read this far in this book, you know by now that any person who's not focused on allowing God to be involved in his or her life will live according to an improper perspective of life. Most of this type of deception can lead to bad habits, addictions, or developing a curse. Remember, the mother curse of all curses is unbelief in Jesus Christ. This kind of existence is not in line with life as God planned it to be. The Bible tells us:

> So it was that when they gave God up and would not even acknowledge him, God gave them up to doing everything their evil minds could think of. Their lives became full of every kind of wickedness and sin, of greed and hate, envy, murder, fighting, lying, bitterness, and gossip.

They were backbiters, haters of God, insolent, proud, braggarts, always thinking of new ways of sinning and continually being disobedient to their parents. They tried to misunderstand, broke their promises, and were heartless—without pity (Rom. 1:28–31 TLB).

Without the pursuit or perseverance of an active relationship with Jesus Christ, a person will have a distorted perspective on life. This in turn blocks the receiving and development of an inspired, God-given vision, and where there is no vision, a person's life is perishing.

The next dream killer is negative people. These can be people who are so-called friends who are pessimistic toward you. They are better known as frenemies, which is the cousin of enemies. They always seem to come up with a reason why you shouldn't do this or that. These people can't comprehend the God-given vision you have because it's not theirs, which makes it difficult for them to fathom how you're going to make it happen. As a result, they belittle you to your face and behind your back.

There can also be people who are around you who are haters because of your progress in life. They envy you for a number of reasons; one may be that they are still stuck under the curse while seeing you free from what had you in bondage. Another might be that when they envy you, they are being dominated by evil spirits and don't even realize it. Whatever the reason or the source, associating with people who are pessimistic, envious, or hateful toward you is a definite dream-killer. Anyone who is not inspiring you to greatness is a dream-killer candidate. You can't share your ideas and visions with just anybody.

The third dream killer is laziness and/or procrastination. A lazy person loves his or her ease, lives in idleness, minds no business, sticks to nothing, brings nothing to pass, and in a particular manner is careless in the business of his or her spiritual condition. Slothfulness is a sure way to poverty or the way to stay in poverty. Laziness is a slow, comfortable path to self-destruction.

I walked by the field of a certain [lazy] fellow and saw that it was overgrown with thorns; it was covered with weeds, and its walls were broken down.

Then, as I looked, I learned this lesson: *"A little extra sleep, A little more slumber, A little folding of the hands to rest"* means that poverty will break in upon you suddenly like a *robber and violently like a bandit* (Prov. 24:30–34 TLB, emphasis mine).

The dream killer "laziness" causes the emotional lack of people's desires to suddenly and surprisingly overtake them in such a powerful way that it will lock them into a strong bondage of passivity. It will increase the discouragement of no hope, and when they talk to other people, they will begin to complain, "I can't do this or I can't do that because of so and so this, and so and so that." Out of ignorance, they will begin to unknowingly prophesy oppression upon themselves that causes them not to progress while having a "dream of wishes" with a heart of pain and not a vision with the energy to pursue it. This also is another way to quench the anointing of the Holy Spirit that's in you.

When you get to the point through prayer, meditation, and soul-searching to get the revelation of how God wired and equipped you with certain potential, that is when you will begin to discover the innate tools that will assist your dream to becoming a physical reality. Keep in mind, though, that the dream I'm discussing is not your personal idea of what you would like to do with your life but God's revelation to you for the assignment He has given you the gift of life on earth for.

I really like the tangible teaching that Pastor Rick Warren of Saddleback church in Orange County, California, uses to give a person insight on how God has wired and shaped him or her. He uses the word "shape" as an acronym to define this concept.

> Whenever God gives us an assignment, he always equips us with what we need to accomplish it. This custom combination of capabilities is called your SHAPE:
>
> **S.** piritual gift(s)
> **H.** eart
> **A.** bilities
> **P.** ersonality
> **E.** xperience
>
> (*Purpose-Driven Life,* pg. 272)

This is an excellent word picture that should help you get a grip on your divine attributes. God has placed within each person a vision that is designed to give purpose and meaning to life. Having a dream or vision is inherently human. You are unique and personally gifted and designed for a purpose.

Bad habits, addictions, and the curse are real-life issues that have to be faced and dealt with in order to soar to your God-given destiny, to clear the way for your purpose in life, and to help your environment and the world become a better place to live for you, your family, and the generations to come.

> And *they that shall be* of thee shall build the old waste places: thou shalt raise up the foundations of many generations; and thou shalt be called, The repairer of the breach, The restorer of paths to dwell in (Isa. 58:12 KJV).

> Where there is no purpose
> Where there is no vision
> Where there is no decision
> The people perish...

Break The Curse Today!

Also by Frank Turner Jr.

Rapture Your Destiny, Who Are You Created to Be?

Frank Turner Jr.'s website:
www.raptureyourdestiny.com

Contact info: frank@raptureyourdestiny.com

PO Box 111271
Nashville, Tennessee 37222